# 10-MINUTE IDEAS
## FOR EARLY YEARS

C000051217

# Nursery rhymes

**Jacquie Finlay, Thérèse Finlay,
Jenni Tavener, Irene Yates**

■ **Quick activities for any time of the day**

■ **Links to Early Learning Goals** ■ **Time-saving photocopiables**

# Credits

**Authors**
Jacquie Finlay
Thérèse Finlay
Jenni Tavener
Irene Yates

**Editor**
Jane Bishop

**Assistant Editor**
Aileen Lalor

**Series Designer**
Anna Oliwa

**Designer**
Erik Ivens

**Cover Illustration**
Craig Cameron/Art
Collection

**Illustrations**
Cathy Hughes

Text © Jacquie Finlay, Thérèse Finlay, Jenni Tavener and Irene Yates, 2005
© 2005 Scholastic Ltd

Published by Scholastic Ltd
Villiers House
Clarendon Avenue
Leamington Spa
Warwickshire
CV32 5PR

www.scholastic.co.uk

Printed by Bell & Bain

1 2 3 4 5 6 7 8 9    5 6 7 8 9 0 1 2 3 4

British Library Cataloguing-in-Publication Data
A catalogue record for this book is available from the British Library.

ISBN 0439-96506-3
ISBN 978-0439-96506-4

The rights of Jacquie Finlay, Thérèse Finlay, Jenni Tavener and Irene Yates to be identified as the authors of this work have been asserted by them in accordance with the Copyright, Designs and Patents Act 1988.

All rights reserved. This book is sold subject to the condition that it shall not, by way of trade or otherwise, be lent, hired out or otherwise circulated without the publisher's prior consent in any form of binding or cover other than that in which it is published and without a similar condition, including this condition, being imposed upon the subsequent purchaser.

No part of this publication may be reproduced, stored in a retrieval system, or transmitted, in any form or by any means, electronic, mechanical, photocopying, recording or otherwise, without the prior permission of the publisher. This book remains copyright, although permission is granted to copy pages where indicated for classroom distribution and use only in the school which has purchased the book, or by the teacher who has purchased the book, and in accordance with the CLA licensing agreement. Photocopying permission is given only for purchasers and not for borrowers of books from any lending service.

# Contents

# Contents

## Old Mother Hubbard

## The Wheels on the Bus

## Photocopiables

# Introduction

Nursery rhymes are an ideal starting point for activities across the curriculum. They can be used to stimulate children's imaginations, and provide many fantastic learning opportunities.

Most children starting playgroup or nursery for the first time will already know a selection of nursery rhymes that they have enjoyed learning at home. Children unfamiliar with nursery rhymes will soon catch up with the constant repetition of rhymes, and they will quickly gain confidence by practising along with the rest of the group.

## Learning through rhymes

The range, repetitive language and rhythms of nursery rhymes provide a solid basis for encouraging early literacy skills.

The rhymes chosen for this book include opportunities for counting ('Five Little Ducks', 'There Were Ten in the Bed'), actions ('Pat-a-cake', 'The Wheels on the Bus') as well as traditional nursery rhymes ('Old Mother Hubbard', 'Hickory, Dickory, Dock'). The themes included offer scope to explore all areas of the curriculum from 'numbers to five' ('Five Little Ducks') to historical contexts ('Old Mother Hubbard'). They offer opportunities to develop musical skills and rhythm through clapping ('Pat-a-cake') and introduce percussion instruments to play alongside the rhyme ('Hickory, Dickory, Dock').

Many simple rhymes are ideal to adapt to a specific topic or theme by changing the words to suit. For example, The Wheels on the Bus can easily become 'The lions in the zoo' for an animal topic, or 'The planes in the sky' to fit in with a transport theme.

The activities in this book are intended to be fun. Just as young children can develop and learn new skills by experimenting with play activities, they can also acquire a range of skills when they play and experiment with language.

## Planning for the Foundation Stage

This book provides activity ideas based on six different popular rhymes, with one chapter for each rhyme. Within the chapter, there are ideas to cover all six Areas of Learning, as set out in the *Curriculum Guidance for the Foundation Stage* (QCA). For each activity, a Stepping Stone and an Early Learning Goal have been selected to enable practitioners to ensure they have comprehensive coverage of all areas. The Area of Learning is provided in an abbreviated form after each Early Learning Goal (see box right).

**PSED** – Personal, social and emotional development

**CLL** – Communication, language and literacy

**MD** – Mathematical development

**KUW** – Knowledge and understanding of the world

**PD** – Physical development

**CD** – Creative development.

## Using this book

The activities in the book are designed to be carried out in a relatively short space of time, with a minimum of preparation. Group sizes vary from two to ten, and

can therefore be used to encourage teamwork and the development of social skills, or independent work and the development of imaginative play and problem solving.

Under 'What you need', a full list of all resources required is given, followed by step-by-step instructions in 'What to do'. Ideas to use with younger children and older children are provided for each activity under the heading 'Support and extension', and at the end of each activity, there are a number of 'Further ideas', which give short suggestions for related ideas and activities.

Copies of the rhymes used in this book are reproduced on photocopiable pages 67 and 68. Pages 69 to 80 provide a range of photocopiable activity sheets linked with specific activity ideas to further extend the children's learning, providing a range of opportunities to develop skills.

## Links with home

At the end of each activity, a 'Home link' offers suggestions as to how parents and carers can help children transfer their developing skills into the home environment. The connection between home and school is a vital one, and parents and carers need to be actively involved in ensuring the continuity of their child's education.

If possible, invite parents and carers in to see and hear the work that the children have completed on nursery rhymes. Encourage the children to recite the rhymes at home with their parents, carers and siblings, and suggest that they tell them about the activities they have enjoyed.

## Assessing the activities

Assessment is a natural part of early years teaching and learning, and will be based on your observations of each child's success at given tasks or in specific situations. As each activity idea has a designated Stepping Stone and Early Learning Goal, it is clear what the expected outcome is and so it is possible to observe whether or not individual children have been successful.

Using the suggestions for supporting or extending children within each activity, it should be clear when a child has achieved a Stepping Stone. A child who is managing an activity without the suggested support, or who is benefiting from the extension ideas, can be viewed as having achieved the appropriate Stepping Stone. Any child who still needs support to carry out the activity can be considered as not having yet mastered that Stepping Stone.

# Five Little Ducks

This popular rhyme can be made into a simple action verse with small or large groups of children. With this series of cross-curricular activities, develop the children's awareness of animals, the environment and changes, and enjoy counting and storytelling.

# A meeting point

## What you need
A copy of the rhyme (page 67); large outdoor plant container (wood, plastic or terracotta); soil; exterior paint; fertiliser; a dwarf evergreen plant; packet of flower seeds (or bedding plants); spare area outside.

## Preparation
Say the rhyme with the children, and talk about where the lost ducks might have gone. How did they find their mother? Ask the children if they have ever been lost. How were they found?

## What to do
Invite the children to help create a plant and flower display to use as a meeting point for children who get separated from their friends at your school, nursery or playgroup. Take the children into the playground to look for a suitable place for their meeting point.

When you have selected an appropriate location, help the children to position their container and to plant their evergreen plant and their seeds or bedding plants. Invite the children to paint or stencil the words 'meeting point' on their container, using exterior paint.

Talk about how the children feel when they are lost or lonely. Ask them questions such as: How can you help someone who is lost or lonely in the playground? Discuss what it feels like to be without a friend to play with. Ask questions such as: How can you help someone who has no one to play with?

## Support and extension
Invite younger children to create a pictorial record of how they set up their meeting point. Encourage older children to create a written record of how they set up their meeting point, illustrating it if they wish.

## Further ideas
■ Care for the flower display by regularly watering, weeding and introducing new plants as the seasons change.
■ Refer back to the rhyme, and invite the children to write an account or draw a picture of where the lost ducks disappeared to, and how they were found.
■ Take photographs of the meeting point in use and display the photographs in a prominent place to inform visitors or newcomers about the resource.

**LEARNING OBJECTIVES**
**STEPPING STONE**
Express needs and feelings in appropriate ways.

**EARLY LEARNING GOAL**
Have a developing awareness of their own needs, views and feelings and be sensitive to the needs, views and feelings of others. (PSED)

**GROUP SIZE**
Small or large groups.

**HOME LINKS**
Ask parents and carers to encourage their children to share their toys with friends, and to take turns when they are playing games together.

# Composing a rhyme

**LEARNING OBJECTIVES**
**STEPPING STONE**
Listen to and join in with stories and poems, one-to-one and also in small groups.

**EARLY LEARNING GOAL**
Explore and experiment with sounds, words and texts. (CLL)

**GROUP SIZE**
Small or large groups.

**HOME LINKS**
Invite parents and carers to look through magazines with their children, to find pictures of animals and their young to share with the group.

## What you need
A copy of the rhyme; pictures and photographs of animals.

## Preparation
If possible, take the children to observe animals on a farm. Otherwise, look together at the pictures and photographs that you have available. Encourage the children to identify the animals they see. Say the rhyme together.

## What to do
Explain to the children that they are going to use their observations of animals to create a new version of the rhyme.

Ask the children to identify the names of baby animals, for example, if you say 'horse', they say 'foal'. How many do they know? What noises do the animals make? Can they demonstrate? Where do these animals live, and what do they eat? Encourage the children to tell you all that they know.

Now ask them to decide what type of baby animal they would like their new rhyme to be about (suggest either lambs, calves or foals for example). Then encourage them to think of a word to describe this animal such as 'lively lambs', 'hungry foals' or 'gentle calves'. Use this as the first line of their rhyme:

'Five gentle calves went out one day…'

Help the children to compose the second line by asking them to think of somewhere that these animals could go, for example, 'through the fields' or 'around the farm', or 'for a walk' and so on. Use this to make the second line of their rhyme:

'Through the fields and far away…'

Next, ask the children what the mother would be called and what noise she would make. Use this information to create the third line:

'Mother cow said moo, moo, moo, moo!'

Finally, help the children to put these ideas together to create the first verse of their 'new' rhyme: 'Five gentle calves went out one day, through the fields and far away, Mother cow said, 'Moo, moo, moo, moo,' and five gentle calves came walking back.'

## Support and extension
Let younger children draw a picture to show the new rhyme. For older children, provide a blank zigzag book for them to record their new rhyme in, using the illustrations to explain the sequence of events. Invite them to write their new rhyme out in the booklet.

## Further ideas
■ Sing other animal rhymes and songs.
■ Help the children to record their new rhymes on a cassette recorder.
■ Paint pictures of animals and their young.

# Comic strip story

### What you need
Paper; pens; coloured pencils; ruler.

### Preparation
Divide an A4 sheet into six equal sections and provide one sheet for each child.

### What to do
Say the rhyme together with the children until you are confident that they understand the sequence of events. Invite them to retell the rhyme using words and pictures.

Talk about the story within the rhyme, and ask questions to stimulate the children's understanding: Where did the little ducks go? How many ducks were there altogether? What did mother duck say? Why did mother duck call the ducklings?

Hand out the grid sheet and explain how to use the squares to retell the story in order. Encourage the children to use both words and pictures to show that they know the sequence of events.

### Support and extension
Let younger children retell the rhyme just using pictures to show the sequence of events. Invite older children to create a new ending or to alter the sequence of events to create a new version of the rhyme.

### Further ideas
■ Make finger-puppet ducks using paper, and use them to retell the rhyme and for counting activities.
■ Encourage the children to use mime to act out the rhyme.
■ Create a comic-strip version of other favourite rhymes or stories.

**LEARNING OBJECTIVES**
**STEPPING STONE**
Begin to be aware of the way stories are structured.

**EARLY LEARNING GOAL**
Retell narratives in the correct sequence, drawing on language patterns of stories. (CLL)

**GROUP SIZE**
Individuals or small groups.

**HOME LINKS**
When parents and carers are sharing rhymes or storybooks with their children, encourage them to ask 'What happens next?' to allow the children to sequence the events.

# Counting wheel

### What you need
The photocopiable sheet 'How many ducks?' on page 69; coloured pens; pencils; scissors; split pins; card; adhesive.

### Preparation
Use the photocopiable sheet to make a model counting wheel as an example. Copy the photocopiable sheet to provide one for each child, and help the children to cut along the dotted lines and to cut around the wheel. These two sections can then be glued onto card.

Help the children to place the wheel behind the window and secure them together using a split pin.

### What to do
Say the rhyme with the children and as you go through it, encourage them to turn their wheel in the direction of the arrows so that the correct number of ducks can be seen in the window. Ask them to count the ducks each time to check that they have the right number. Can they guess how many ducks they will see next time?

Ask questions to inspire mathematical awareness, for example: If I start with one duck and add two more, how many ducks are there altogether? Start with five ducks, count back four ducks, how many are left? Start at five ducks and count backwards until all the ducks have gone. Encourage the children to use the correct mathematical terms, such as more/less than.

Use the wheel to inspire mathematical activities such as counting on and counting back, ordering, sequencing, and addition and subtraction up to five.

### Support and extension
For younger children, enlarge the photocopiable page and stick the components onto stiff card if possible. Make one large wheel to use with a group of children. Invite older children to draw five extra ducks in the pond and use the wheel to inspire mathematical activities up to ten.

### Further ideas
■ Create a three-dimensional scene about the rhyme using ducks made from Plasticine, clay or dough, on a pond made using aluminium foil lining a shallow box.
■ Create a number line from zero to ten on the theme of ducks.
■ Look at some famous paintings that show animals or birds.

**LEARNING OBJECTIVES**
**STEPPING STONE**
Enjoy joining in with number rhymes and songs.

**EARLY LEARNING GOAL**
Count reliably up to 10 everyday objects. (MD)

**GROUP SIZE**
Small groups.

**HOME LINKS**
Suggest that parents and carers use mathematical language as their children play at home, inviting them to count their soft toys or to add and then take away toys from a group.

# Swimming ducks

## What you need
Selection of small and large boxes; card; adhesive; table tennis balls or counters; paints; sticky paper; selection of commercial number games.

## What to do
Encourage the children to play some simple number games such as dominoes, snakes and ladders and number snap.

Next, provide each child with one large box (mother duck) and five smaller boxes (the baby ducks). Show them how to stick the boxes onto a card base in a long line, with the large box at the front. Help the children to cut out one large duck shape and five small duck shapes from card or sticky paper. Attach these to the sides of the six boxes to represent a line of swimming ducks.

Help the children to write a number (in numeral form) on or beside each box (select the numbers used according to the age and ability of your children). When complete, the children can try to throw a ball or counter into the boxes. They can then add up their total score and write it down. Let them play several times and see what is their highest score.

Afterwards, ask the children to explain how they made their game. Ask questions such as: What are your rules and instructions? What was your highest or lowest score? Discuss with the children ways of making their game easier or more complicated.

## Support and extension
Limit the number of boxes used and label the boxes with dots (instead of figures) for younger children to count. Provide a duck template for them to draw around. Invite older children to make their game more challenging by writing addition or subtraction signs next to the numbers by their boxes for them to add or to take away from their running total.

## Further ideas
■ Encourage the children to play their game with a friend. They can write down each other's score and compare their results after each game.
■ Record the rules and instructions for their game in writing.
■ Let the children design and make a two-dimensional board game using numbers, dice and counters.
■ Encourage the children to play playground counting games, such as hopscotch or 'What's the time Mr Wolf?.

---

**LEARNING OBJECTIVES**
**STEPPING STONE**
Recognise numerals 1 to 5, then 1 to 9.

**EARLY LEARNING GOAL**
Recognise numerals 1 to 9. (MD)

**GROUP SIZE**
Individuals or small groups.

**HOME LINKS**
Make your number games available for children to borrow to play with their parents, carers or siblings.

# The little ducks' journey

## LEARNING OBJECTIVES
**STEPPING STONE**
Describe a simple journey.

## EARLY LEARNING GOAL
Use everyday words to describe position. (MD)

## GROUP SIZE
Individuals or small groups.

## What you need
A copy of the rhyme; paper (30cm × 60cm); paints and painting equipment (or coloured pens, pencils, crayons and pastels).

## What to do
Say the rhyme together and encourage the children to imagine the little ducks' journey from their mother's pond to the 'hills and far away'. Ask them to consider what the ducks might see on their journey. Provide some suggestions to inspire their imagination such as: 'out of the pond, through a field, along a road, across a river, under a bridge and over the hills'.

Next, invite the children to paint or draw a map showing the ducks' imaginary journey. Suggest that they begin their picture on the left-hand side of the page by drawing the duck pond, and finish their picture on the right hand side of the page with a drawing of the 'hills far away'. Encourage the children to include three or more features between these two landmarks for the ducks to go 'over', 'around', 'through' or 'across'.

Encourage the children to describe their route maps. Ask open questions and enquiries such as: Tell me about the ducks' route to the hills, what did the ducks go over, round or through? Can you describe the ducks' route home? Encourage the children to use the correct vocabulary and reinforce it by showing you with their hands 'through' and 'over'.

## Support and extension
Invite younger children to cut out and colour five little ducks and one mother duck from thin card (using a template made by an adult if necessary). Let them secure their ducks along the map to illustrate where the ducks travelled. Encourage older children to cut out some shapes from thin white card to represent signposts, which they can label with the different destinations on their maps – 'to the field', 'to the river' or 'to the hills'. The children can then position their signposts on their map in the appropriate places to show the route taken by the ducks.

## Further ideas
■ Can the children describe a journey that is familiar to them, such as their journey home, to the park or to the shops?
■ Invite the children to draw or paint a route map showing some of the main features they encounter on their way home.
■ Ask the children to act out a journey using obstacles and body movements.
■ Read *Rosie's Walk* by Pat Hutchins (Picture Puffin) which reinforces the terms 'over', 'under', 'round' and 'through'.

## HOME LINKS
Ask parents and carers to talk with their children about their routes to your setting. Invite the children to tell you how they get there, using as much positional language as you can encourage.

# Hook-a-duck game

## What you need
Low table; drape (various shades of green); green card; scissors; two dowelling rods; small box/bucket; shiny blue paper (or foil); six identical plastic ducks; paper; paints and brushes; aprons; stapler; sticky labels; sticky tape; six strips of non-fraying fabric (15cm × 2cm) folded to create a loop.

## Preparation
Cover a low table in a green drape. Let the children help to cut several strips of green card to resemble thick blades of grass, attach these to the edge of the table. Invite the children to cut a large 'duck pond' from shiny paper and put it in the centre of the table. Ask the children to paint a background scene showing 'hills far away'. Mount the scenery onto a display board or wall behind the table. Attach a loop of fabric to the back of the six ducks using strong sticky tape.

## What to do
Ask the children to help make the 'hook a duck' game. Place a number label on to the base of the six plastic ducks (vary the numbers to suit the level of your group). Encourage the children to use the interactive display to play the following games:

**Game 1:** Take turns to hook up two or more ducks using the rods. Add the score. Replace the ducks. The highest score wins. Play again, but this time, the lowest score wins.

**Game 2:** Hook two ducks. Take the lowest number away from the highest number. The winner is the player with the highest score.

Afterwards, ask questions such as: What is your highest score? How many ducks do you need to hook to get a score of more than three? Can you make up a new game? Tell me the rules of your new game.

## Support and extension
Help younger children to add up their scores. Invite older children to write the rules and instructions for the games.

## Further idea
■ Add five cardboard or plastic fish to the 'pond', attach a fabric loop to the top of each fish and 'plus' or 'minus' signs to the underside of each fish.

**LEARNING OBJECTIVES**

**STEPPING STONE**
Show an interest in number problems.

**EARLY LEARNING GOAL**
Begin to relate addition to combining two groups of objects and subtraction to 'taking away'. (MD)

**GROUP SIZE**
Small groups.

**HOME LINKS**
Let the children invite their parents and carers in to your group to play the games with them.

# Animal book

## LEARNING OBJECTIVES
**STEPPING STONE**
Examine objects and living things to find out more about them.

## EARLY LEARNING GOAL
Find out about, and identify, some features of living things, objects and events they observe. (KUW)

## GROUP SIZE
Individuals or small groups.

### What you need
The photocopiable sheet 'Mothers and babies' on page 70; A4 paper; a stapler and staples; coloured pens; pencils; adhesive; scissors.

### Preparation
If possible, take the children to visit the animals in a local farm and help them to name and identify various animals. If a visit is not possible, look at some illustrated information books together to observe different animals. Copy the photocopiable sheet for each child. Make a blank booklet for each child by dividing an A4 sheet of paper into four equal sections. Fold these sections in half and staple together along the folded edge to create a small booklet with four pages.

### What to do
Find out what the children know about animals and their young by asking questions such as: What will a puppy grow up into? What is a baby duck called? Talk about the similarities and differences between the appearance of the various adult animals and their young.

Provide each child with a copy of the photocopiable sheet and the pre-prepared small four page booklet. Invite them to write their name on the front page and decorate it in their own design.

Invite the children to cut along the dotted lines on their photocopiable sheet to produce 14 small pictures. Let them sort and match the pictures into seven pairs showing seven mothers and their young. Encourage the children to stick their pictures into their booklet in the appropriate pairs.

### Support and extension
Use the individual pictures for matching and sorting games to help younger children become familiar with the names of the different adult and young animals. With older children, use two sheets of A4 to make an eight page booklet. Invite the children to use the extra pages to record relevant information that they have discovered about the various animals such as food and habitat.

### Further ideas
■ Find out about the young of other animals such as zoo animals and wild animals and birds.
■ Paint or draw pictures of animals from firsthand observations, such as birds in the park or playground, a rabbit in a 'run' or a fish in a tank.
■ Visit a pet shop with the children, or invite someone to bring their pet in to see the children.
■ Ask children to write a story, or draw a cartoon strip, about an adventure with their favourite animal.

## HOME LINKS
Make additional copies of the photocopiable sheet and let the children take them home to play matching games with their families.

# Roundabout books

## What you need
The story of the *Ugly Duckling* by Hans Christian Anderson (Ladybird); pictures or photographs of eggs, cygnets and adult swans; paper (15cm × 45cm); coloured pens and pencils; a visit to view swans or ducks in their natural habitat (optional); information books.

## What to do
Talk about how all birds hatch from eggs, and, if possible, visit a pond to view ducks and swans. Alternatively, use information books to show the children relevant pictures.

Next, read the story of the *Ugly Duckling* to the children and show them the pictures of the eggs, cygnets and swans to name and identify. Encourage the children to observe the similarities and differences between the pictures and place them in order of age.

Provide each child with a strip of paper, and help them to fold it into three equal sections to produce a three page zigzag book. Invite them to draw a picture of the egg, cygnet and swan in order of age on the three pages. Finally, help the children to fasten the first and last pages together to create a triangular 'roundabout' book.

Use the roundabout book to highlight the fact that the egg, chick, bird sequence is a continuous process. Invite the children to draw arrows on each page to indicate the sequence of events.

Discuss what happened to the cygnet as it grew into an adult. Ask: What happened to the cygnet's neck as time went by? What animals change as they grow up?

## Support and extension
Work with a group of younger children to create one large 'roundabout' book to share. Invite older children to write explanatory labels on the pages of their zigzag or 'roundabout' book such as 'an egg hatches into a cygnet', 'a cygnet grows into a swan', 'a swan lays an egg'.

## Further ideas
■ Encourage the children to retell the story of the *Ugly Duckling* in their own words, changing the characters or setting if they wish.
■ Invite the children to sketch swans using white chalk on black paper.
■ Help the children to draw around their hands on white paper. Cut out the shapes with the children and use them as feathers to create a swan collage.

**LEARNING OBJECTIVES**
**STEPPING STONE**
Begin to differentiate between past and present.

**EARLY LEARNING GOAL**
Find out about past and present events in their own lives, and in those of their families and other people they know. (KUW)

**GROUP SIZE**
Any size

**HOME LINKS**
Invite parents and carers to accompany the children on a visit to see ducks or swans in their natural habitat.

# Making music

### What you need
A selection of percussion instruments; a comfortable place to sit; cassette player and blank cassette (optional).

### What to do
Sing some familiar nursery rhymes and songs with the children and invite them to use the selection of percussion instruments to accompany their singing.

Discuss the names and sounds of different instruments and talk about the similarities and differences between the instruments. Ask: What is the difference between a tambour and a tambourine? How many different ways can you play a cymbal? What different sounds can you make using a drum?

Next, say the 'Five Little Ducks' rhyme together and encourage the children to use the percussion instruments to help them make up a simple tune to accompany the words. Allow them time to experiment by using trial and error to discover sounds and tunes which they enjoy listening to.

Depending on the age of your children, you may need to help them to develop controlled use of the instruments and to take turns to play!

If there is an opportunity, let the children record their music to hear again or to play to an audience of other children, visitors or parents.

### Support and extension
Encourage younger children to consider and identify factors such as soft and loud music and fast and slow rhythms. With older children, introduce terms such as 'tone', 'pitch' and 'rhythm'.

### Further ideas
■ Listen to the music of *Peter and the Wolf* (Prokofiev) and find out which instruments represent each animal.
■ Make your own percussion instruments using reclaimed materials such as tins, cardboard boxes and offcuts of wood.
■ Play recordings of the children's favourite animal songs, and let the children dance, sing and play their own instruments in time to the recordings.

---

**LEARNING OBJECTIVES**

**STEPPING STONE**
Explore the different sounds of instruments.

**EARLY LEARNING GOAL**
Recognise and explore how sounds can be changed, sing simple songs from memory, recognise repeated sounds and sound patterns and match movements to music. (CD)

**GROUP SIZE**
Small groups.

**HOME LINKS**
Suggest that parents and carers use recycled materials to make percussion instruments with their children, for example, putting some dried beans in a yoghurt pot and taping on a lid to make a shaker.

---

# Hickory, Dickory, Dock

This rhyme provides opportunities to consider what happens at different times of the day, establishing a basis for telling the time and developing language and communication skills. By taking notice of the mouse in the rhyme, children can explore habitats, colours and textures.

## Don't run away!

### What you need
Card; drawing and writing materials.

### Preparation
Draw and cut out a large card mouse shape.

### What to do
This is a discussion-based activity where you can encourage the children to participate as both speakers and listeners. Attempt to ensure all children have something to contribute, but be sensitive to any children who are unwilling to disclose too much personal detail.

Ask the children how they think the mouse felt when the clock struck one. Do they think he was surprised or shocked, for example? Ask the children if they can change their facial expressions to show different emotions for the other children to guess the feeling expressed. See if they can all make faces to show anger, shock, horror and happiness.

Choose one child to make an expression and another to name it. Then ask this child to recall a time when they may have felt like this. Repeat this several times, until different feelings and emotions have been discussed. Scribe these feelings on the large mouse shape, with drawings to depict the emotion.

Invite the children to discuss which of these emotions they like to feel, which they don't and why. Talk about what helps them to recover from these sad or nasty feelings. Choose a child to retell an event, without naming which emotion they felt. See if the other children can guess the emotion.

### Support and extension
With younger children, centre the discussion around events that have made the children happy or sad, encouraging them to talk about how they felt and why. Encourage older children to write an account of a time when they felt a strong emotion. Consider with the children how other people have strong emotions and that these should be respected.

### Further ideas
■ Make a 'Face book' with each page depicting a different feeling/emotion.
■ Make a double-sided face attached to a ruler, with two distinct expressions shown, such as happy one side and sad the other, or angry and calm.

**LEARNING OBJECTIVES**
**STEPPING STONE**
Express needs and feelings in appropriate ways.

**EARLY LEARNING GOAL**
Have a developing awareness of their own needs, views and feelings and be sensitive to the needs, views and feelings of others. (PSED)

**GROUP SIZE**
Small groups.

**HOME LINKS**
Suggest that parents and carers talk with their children about how they are feeling as they play, taking the opportunity to stress how it is kind to play fairly and share toys with their friends.

# Where did he go?

### What you need
White paper; sugar paper; pencils; colouring materials; felt-tipped pens; large sheet of card; enlarged copy of the nursery rhyme (page 67); toy mouse or a picture of a mouse; clock.

### Preparation
Cut out and make a book in the shape of a clock for each child, using white paper with a sugar-paper cover. On the large sheet of card, draw and cut out a clock to use as a visual aid. Display the nursery rhyme.

### What to do
Show the children the clock and mouse and ask if these objects remind them of a nursery rhyme. Once they have guessed which rhyme you mean, recite 'Hickory dickory dock' together and discuss with the children where they think the mouse went, and how he got there.

Ask the children: What type of clock was it? How did the mouse get inside? Is the clock big or little? How big was the mouse? Where did the mouse live? What did the mouse like to do?

Next, ask the children to imagine they are a mouse and to think about the different places they could run to. Show the children the large segmented clock you have drawn, and invite them to draw pictures in the segments, to show where the mouse may run to. Let the children suggest suitable places (shops, park and so on). Discuss the options they suggest, and ask them whether the mouse would like the place, how long it would take and so on.

Finally, ask the children to record in their own books the mouse's journeys, drawing pictures or writing their ideas.

### Support and extension
Develop younger children's positional language by asking them to place a mouse in different places on the large cardboard clock with their pictures on ('next to the swings', 'behind the shops' and so on). Encourage the children to act out the nursery rhyme. Encourage older children to create their own nursery rhyme books, starting with other rhyming phrases such as 'Yickerty, yackerty, yak'. The children may also enjoy miming where the mouse went, asking other children to guess.

### Further ideas
■ Create a word bank, displaying the words on mice shapes around a clock.
■ Make a collection of different types of clocks – alarm clocks, stop-watches and so on. Discuss what they are used for.

---

### LEARNING OBJECTIVES
**STEPPING STONE**
Use words and/or gestures, including body language such as eye contact and facial expression, to communicate.

### EARLY LEARNING GOAL
Interact with others, negotiating plans and activities and taking turns in conversation. (CLL)

### GROUP SIZE
Small groups.

### HOME LINKS
Encourage parents and carers to share other nursery rhymes with their children, inviting them to recall what happens in the rhymes afterwards.

# What's the time Mr Mouse?

## What you need
Paper; writing materials; copy of the nursery rhyme; three coloured circles of card; rulers; Sellotape.

## Preparation
Draw a grandfather clock on a piece of paper and copy one for each child. Label each of the circles: morning, afternoon, evening and attach each circle to a ruler.

## What to do
Choose three children to each hold one of the rulers with the circles attached. Invite another child to mime an activity which they complete during the day, such as eating breakfast, getting washed, playing with friends, reading or going to bed.

Let the other children guess what activity the child is acting out. Once someone has guessed, ask the children in which part of the day the activity normally takes place. When this has been identified, ask the child holding the appropriate circle to lift it in the air. Repeat this game with different children three or four times.

Discuss with the children each of the activities in detail – how they are performed, with whom and when. Encourage the children to talk about why these activities take place at different times during the day. Ask: Why do we sleep at night-time? What is your favourite time of the day? When do you get up? What time do you eat?

Next ask the children to place the activities in sequential order, beginning with the things that are completed earliest in the day.

Introduce the picture of the grandfather clock to the children, and ask them to record activities on the clock face in the order in which they happen.

## Support and extension
With younger children, limit the number of activities, and focus on morning and evening to begin with. Let the children draw pictures of activities related to these times of the day. With older children, use a clock to demonstrate the time that each activity took place during the day. Introduce the term 'o'clock', and encourage the children to try and mime a suitable activity for each hour of the day.

## Further ideas
■ Sing 'Here we go Round the Mulberry Bush', inserting the activities which the children have selected, for example 'This is the way we brush our teeth', or 'This is the way we eat our lunch'.
■ Play a game using actions appropriate to the time shown on the clock. So when the clock shows 8 o'clock, the children stretch to wake up and so on.
■ Make a daily timetable in the form of a clock, and move a mouse to each activity as it occurs.

**LEARNING OBJECTIVES**
**STEPPING STONE**
Use talk, actions and objects to recall and relive past experiences.

**EARLY LEARNING GOAL**
Use language to imagine and recreate roles and experiences. (CLL)

**GROUP SIZE**
Small groups.

**HOME LINKS**
Ask parents and carers to point out the different times of the day to their children, 'It's morning now, time to get up', 'It's the afternoon so it's time to go to playgroup' and so on.

# Tick 2 3, tock 2 3

### What you need
The photocopiable sheet 'Reach the clock' on page 71; writing and colouring materials; card; toy mouse or a picture of a mouse.

### Preparation
Cut out ten paw prints from card and label them with the numbers 1–10. Make copies of the photocopiable sheet to provide one per child.

### What to do
Practise counting up to ten with the children using different methods to count, including clapping hands, tapping knees, stamping feet and nodding their heads.

Show the children the paw prints with the numbers on, and ask them whether they recognise the numbers. As each number is held up, ask the children to clap that number of times.

Ask ten children to stand up and give them a paw print to hold. Ask them to name their numbers. Invite the other children to say if the children holding the numbers are in the correct order. If they are not, ask them which number should come first, second, third and so on. Encourage the standing children to re-position themselves accordingly.

Place the paw prints in sequence on the floor as a number line. Choose a child to hold the mouse and make it jump from paw print to paw print, counting as it goes.

Show the photocopiable sheet to the children, explaining that the mouse has to get to the clock by jumping on the footprints in the correct order. Encourage the children to use a pencil to draw a path to the clock joining up the paw prints.

### Support and extension
Restrict the activity to numbers up to five with younger children. Invite the children to use the paw print number line as a general resource and encourage them to move along the numbers in different ways, such as hops and jumps. Encourage older children to begin the number line at different places – to start at 6 and count up to 10, for example. You could extend the number line and invite older children to count up in twos, fives and tens.

### Further ideas
■ Use the number line for practical addition: The mouse is on number 2. He jumps three prints. What number is he on now?
■ Highlight odd and even numbers on a number line which goes beyond ten.
■ Create more dot-to-dot pictures for other children to complete.

### LEARNING OBJECTIVES
**STEPPING STONE**
Say the number after any number up to 9.

**EARLY LEARNING GOAL**
Say and use number names in order infamiliar contexts. (MD)

### GROUP SIZE
Small or large groups.

### HOME LINKS
Ask parents and carers to take every opportunity to talk to their children about numbers which they see when they are out and about, including odd and even numbers, numbers on doors, telephone numbers, their ages, how many days there are in each month, and how many months in the year.

# Bumpy, lumpy, soft

## What you need
Paper; writing and colouring materials; set rings; a selection of textured resources (sandpaper, tissue paper, stone, cotton wool, fruit, candles, wood, Cellophane, coloured foil, aluminium foil, sponge, foam, soft ball, plastic bag, book); completed 'Touchy, feely clock' display, described on page 24.

## Preparation
You will need to complete the display on page 24 first. Gather the children around the display and talk about the different textures they can see and feel on the clock. Arrange the selection of resources on the carpet in front of the children.

## What to do
As this is a discussion-based activity, provide opportunities for all the children to develop and extend their understanding and vocabulary.

Choose an object and begin by using one word to describe it without actually naming the object. Pass it round to all the children in turn, and ask each child to think of a different word/phrase to describe it. For example, if you choose a candle, the children may suggest: smooth; circles at each end; rolls; cold; hard; you light it and so on.

Next, place all the objects in front of the children, and choose one child at a time to describe an object without touching or naming it. However, this time, the other children have to guess the object being described.

Introduce the word 'opposite' to the children, and explain its meaning, giving examples. Choose one child to pick an object and describe one of its properties. Ask another child to choose an object which has an opposite property. If the first child chooses a wooden block, the second could choose a sponge, or children could contrast a plastic bag with some aluminium foil.

Encourage the children to use the range of resources to sort and classify the items into a variety of sets. Let the children record the sets.

## Support and extension
Let younger children make a 'feely book' by sticking in different textured materials. Create simple sets – for example, all soft items or all hard. With older children, discuss the differences between natural and manufactured materials, considering the properties of both. Look at the different processes used to extract natural materials, such as making paper from wood.

## Further ideas
■ Use a 'feely bag' to guess the different objects by touch.
■ Test if it is possible to use other senses to guess or describe an object.
■ Make models using different textured materials.

**LEARNING OBJECTIVES**
**STEPPING STONE**
Examine objects and living things to find out more about them.

**EARLY LEARNING GOAL**
Investigate objects and materials by using all of their senses as appropriate. (KUW)

**GROUP SIZE**
Small groups.

**HOME LINKS**
Ask each child to bring in an item with an interesting texture from home to use in the activity.

# Open the door

## LEARNING OBJECTIVES
### STEPPING STONE
Construct with a purpose in mind, using a variety of resources.

### EARLY LEARNING GOAL
Select the tools and techniques they need to shape, assemble and join materials they are using. (KUW)

## GROUP SIZE
Small groups.

### What you need
A4 pieces of card; drawing and colouring materials; Sellotape; adhesive; paperclips; split pins; ribbon; treasury tags; hole-punch; Blu-Tack; scissors; table covering; aprons; examples of flap books.

### Preparation
Cover the work surface and make the resources accessible to the children.

### What to do
Look with the children at different hinges – beginning by showing them some flap books. Discuss why these books have flaps, how they work and how they are attached.

Talk to the children about where they could find hinges, what they are made from, and what purpose they serve. Discuss clocks that have hinged doors and the workings contained behind them. The children could consider the different purposes and constructions of doors. Ask them: What are they made from? How do they open? What type of handles do they have? Do they lock? Can you see through them?

Show the children a selection of resources, explaining that these can be used in different ways to make a hinge to go on a clock, like the one in 'Hickory dickory dock'.

Demonstrate on a piece of A4 card how the resources can be used to make hinges. Use the correct names for the resources (ribbon, Sellotape, treasury tags) and discuss where they will put their door. Let the children draw and cut out a circle of card for a clock face, which they can colour and complete including all features. Attach the clock face to a piece of A4 card.

Next, let them cut out a piece of card as a door, which they can attach to the A4 card base using whichever method they choose as a hinge. Encourage the children to each decide upon the best hinge and the best point and method of attachment.

Complete the clocks by drawing a mouse and pendulum and sticking them behind the door.

### Support and extension
For younger children, provide a pre-cut clock face and door for them to attach, and limit the selection of resources from which they can choose. Invite older children to make individual flap books using hinges, to enhance the rhyme. They could use the hinged flaps to hide the mouse in different pictures, such as behind a tree, in the park and so on.

## HOME LINKS
Ask parents and carers to help their children to make a hinge search around their homes and to tell the other children at your group what they found.

### Further ideas
■ Look at levers and how they are used in books. Try and include them in models that you make.
■ Investigate how cogs work. Use construction kits to make your own model using a cog mechanism.

# Playing in the past

## What you need
Selection of toys (suitable for babies, young children and older children); sack; paper; card; writing and drawing materials; bag; selection of baby equipment (clothes, toys, feeding bottles, food).

## Preparation
Make labels saying 'Past', 'Present' and 'Future'. Place all the toys in a large sack. Place all the baby equipment in a large bag. Fold card into three sections, labelled 'Past', 'Present' and 'Future'.

## What to do
Explain to the children that you have found a bag and you need their help to work out who it belongs to. Empty the bag containing the baby equipment out onto the floor and discuss each article.

Encourage the children to decide who the bag belongs to and why. Suggest to them that *they* would not use the things in the bag any more. Ask the children to talk about something they did as a baby that they don't do now.

Next, bring in the toy sack and choose a child to pick out a toy. Ask: Would you like to play with this toy? Help them to think about when they could play with it, introducing the words past, present and future. Set out the 'Past', 'Present' and 'Future' labels on the floor and ask the children to select a toy and place it in the correct set. Explain that you want to show whether they would have played with it as a baby, now, or when they are older. Introduce phrases to reinforce the concept of time: in the olden days; a long time ago; now; when you grow up.

Finish by providing each child with a folded piece of card. Ask them to draw a toy from their own past, present and future, to create a toy timeline.

## Support and extension
Focus on the practical side of this activity with younger children giving them opportunities to sort a variety of toys and games into sets. Develop their historical language, including vocabulary such as old/new/past/present and future. Encourage older children to make timelines of events in their own lives, using drawings or photographs. Let them try playing games which their parents, grandparents or great-grandparents might have played, such as 'Oranges and lemons', 'Whip and top', and so on.

## Further ideas
■ Display other timelines showing photographs of the children throughout the year or to show the changes in seasons.
■ Consider changes between past and present in a particular area such as school life or transport.

---

**LEARNING OBJECTIVES**
**STEPPING STONE**
Begin to differentiate between past and present.

**EARLY LEARNING GOAL**
Find out about past and present events in their own lives, and in those of their families and other people they know. (KUW)

**GROUP SIZE**
Small groups.

**HOME LINKS**
Ask children to talk to their parents and carers about what sort of nursery rhymes they might have sung, including 'Hickory, Dickory, Dock'. Ask them to find out what toys their parents and grandparents might have played with and to compare these with their own.

# Touchy feely clock

## LEARNING OBJECTIVES

**STEPPING STONE**
Show curiosity, observe and manipulate objects.

**EARLY LEARNING GOAL**
Investigate objects and materials by using all of their senses as appropriate. (KUW)

## GROUP SIZE
Small groups.

## What you need
Sandpaper; felt; fabric; paper; card; coloured Cellophane; shiny paper; pipe cleaners; paint; chalk; PVA glue; crayons; felt-tipped pens; aprons; scissors; brushes; wool; string; polystyrene pieces; split pins; sponges; table covering; large copy of the nursery rhyme.

## Preparation
Cut card into circles. Cut numbers 1–12 out of different textures and stick onto card. Cover the work surfaces

## What to do
Ask the children to work in groups on the following tasks:
**Face of clock** – prepare the background to the numbers by sponge-printing a large circle. Attach card with split pins to the centre of the face to make the clock hands.
**Base of clock** – draw a large grandfather clock shape. Use brown paint and PVA glue mixed together. Brush/comb through to create a wood effect.
**Pendulum** – make two contrasting pendulums, cover one in coloured foil and the other with matt paper. Attach these to the clock base using split pins.
**Mice** – using the cut circles of card, cut each to the centre and fold to make a cone shape to form mice heads. Add mice features using pipe cleaners and pieces of fabric.

Once all of the parts are complete, assemble the display by gluing the numbers onto the clock face. Position the face on the wall, with the clock base underneath. Arrange the mouse heads on and around the clock, and display a copy of the rhyme.

## Support and extension
Ask younger children questions about the material numbers on the clocks inviting them to say which is the softest, hardest or fluffiest number. Ask older children for their ideas to make the display better, inviting them to think of ways to make the mouse run up the clock, or make the pendulums move.

The clock struck one.

Hands made from card.

Sponge painted circle.

Use combs to get wood grain effect.

Mice made from circles of card shaped into cones.

Hickory dickory dock

## HOME LINKS
Ask parents and carers to try some junk modelling with their children at home, using everyday resources and craft materials to create simple models.

## Further ideas
■ Make clock faces out of paper plates. Ask a child to set the clock to a certain time, and then ask the others to mime an appropriate activity.
■ Invent new things for the mouse to do at different times: 'the clock struck three and the mouse had tea'; 'the clock struck eight and the mouse opened the gate'.

# Clap your hands

## What you need
A beater to act as a baton.

## Preparation
Explain to the children that when the baton is held up they must stop immediately. Tell them to make sure they watch the baton at all times.

## What to do
Begin by clapping a rhythm and encourage the children to copy. Start with a simple rhythm and then quickly progress to a more complex one. For example, start with one slow clap, through to one slow and two fast claps.

Once this has been mastered, explain to the children that they are going to clap out their own name. Clap out each child's name in turn and let the children copy. Following this, you should clap together the word 'hickory', using the baton to show the children when to start and stop.

Split the group into two, one group still clapping 'hickory' and the other, 'dickory' – but only when the baton commands!

Now separate the children into three groups and ask each small group to clap 'hickory', 'dickory', or 'dock'. Again, the three groups must perform only when the baton signals to them.

Now invite the children to join you to clap out the whole nursery rhyme. Select a small number of children to tap on their knees the rhythm of 'tick tock'. Tell these children to continue the 'tick tock' rhythm while the rest of the group clap the rhythm of the whole nursery rhyme.

Discuss with the children the difference between fast and slow claps. Talk about other ways to represent the rhythm, apart from clapping, such as using percussion instruments. What else can we tap to the rhythm? Can we wave our arms to the rhythm? Can we bang the drum fast or slow? Do you think the mouse runs fast or slow?

## Support and extension
Show the baton to the younger children and use it to direct them into clapping out a fast or slow rhythm. Initially, hold the baton high for fast, lowering it for slow. Experiment with the baton, moving it quickly for a fast rhythm and slowly for slow clapping. Let the children take it in turns to conduct with the baton. With older children, use the nursery rhyme and the work on rhythms to create a round with the children. Introduce some percussion instruments, such as a tambourine or chime bars, to develop simple rhythmic patterns.

## Further ideas
■ Make a musical score by drawing a mouse, a pendulum clock and an alarm clock. Children can take turns to be the conductor and point to each of the pictures, while the rest of the class perform
■ Use a range of different musical instruments to make sound effects that complement the rhyme.

**LEARNING OBJECTIVES**
**STEPPING STONE**
Respond to rhythm, music and story by means of gesture and movement.

**EARLY LEARNING GOAL**
Move with confidence, imagination and in safety. (PD)

**GROUP SIZE**
Large groups.

**HOME LINKS**
Suggest that parents and carers help their children to clap out words at home starting with their name, or names of their pets.

# What colour's your mouse?

**LEARNING OBJECTIVES**
**STEPPING STONE**
Explore what happens when they mix colours.

**EARLY LEARNING GOAL**
Explore colour, texture, shape, form and space in two or three dimensions. (CD)

■■■■■■■■■■

**GROUP SIZE**
Small groups.

■■■■■■■■■■

## What you need
*Mouse Paint* by Ellen Stoll Walsh (Orchard Books); paper; powder paint (yellow, red, blue); paintbrushes; water; spatulas; aprons; table covering; containers; spoons; sponges; mixing palettes; elastic; card; finger paints.

## Preparation
Cut the card into five mouse faces and attach elastic sufficient to fit a child's wrist. Cover the work surface and put finger paints in containers on the table. Ask the children to put on aprons. Prepare the painting equipment by placing a spatula in each pot of powder paint, filling two containers with water, placing a spoon in each and dampening a sponge. (Ready mix paint can also be used. Place this in small containers.)

## What to do
Read *Mouse Paint* to the children. This is a story about some mice who get paint on their feet, then dance in different coloured paint to mix a new colour. Choose one child to be the mouse by placing the mouse face on the child's wrist. As you read the story, emphasise the colours of the mice. When you reach the first colour mix in the book (a red mouse in a yellow puddle), ask the children to predict what they think will happen to the paint. Explain to the 'mouse' child that they are going to copy the mouse in the story by jumping in the red paint and then dancing in the yellow, using fingers to represent the mouse's feet.

Let the child try this and check with the story that the same colour has been made. Repeat the process, choosing a different child for each colour mix.

Once you have read through the whole story, place the equipment on the table and give each child a palette and a brush. Explain that they can mix their own paints by placing a spatula of powder paint on their palette and a spoonful of water, mixing it together with the brush. After the three primary colours have been mixed, let the children create new colours on their palettes or on paper. Encourage the children to wash their equipment after they have finished painting.

## Support and extension
Before introducing younger children to mixing powder paints, provide plenty of opportunity for them to experiment using ready-mixed finger paints. With older children, introduce black and white powder paint, discussing the effects when these are mixed with primary colours. Make colour shade charts, checked, striped or spiral.

■■■■■■■■■■■■■■■■■■■■■■■■■■■■■■■■■■■■■■■■■

**HOME LINKS**
Send copies of the rhyme home, and ask parents and carers to help their children learn it.

■■■■■■■■■■

## Further ideas
■ Make camouflage pictures, choosing one shade for the background and a shade darker or lighter for the object on top.
■ Show some examples of the work of a colourful artist such as Jackson Pollock, Andy Warhol or Roy Lichtenstein.

# There Were Ten in the Bed

Inspire the children's sense of fun and imagination with these ideas to explore the theme of bedtime, including designing a fantasy bedroom, finding out about animals' sleeping habits, and composing a lullaby. These activities are particularly useful in improving children's hygiene.

## My favourite bedtime toy

### What you need
The children's own bedtime toys (provide some spare soft toys too).

### What to do
Invite the children to bring in a bedtime toy (or other favourite toy). Have some spare soft toys in case any children forget to bring their own in.

As a circle-time activity, invite the children to show in turn their chosen toy to the rest of the group. Encourage them to tell their friends what the toy is called, who gave it to them and to explain why it is special to them. Children who have chosen a toy from your collection could describe the toy and say why they have chosen it.

Encourage the children to wait for their turn to speak and to listen carefully to what their friends are saying.

After circle time, let the children take their toys to play with them as they try out the various activities in your group. Invite them to share the toys together inviting the toys to 'play' together. Talk about how nice it is to play together sharing the toys.

### Support and extension
With younger children, use a variety of prompts to encourage them to talk about their favourite toy. Emphasise the importance of listening to others and of making turns to speak to ask questions. Encourage older children to work in pairs with two toys, and to compare the physical attributes of the toys talking about the similarities and differences between them.

### Further ideas
■ Look at the pictures together, and read aloud the stories by Jane Hissey about *Old Bear* (Beaver Books).
■ Provide a safe place for the children to leave their special soft toys so that they don't get damaged during their visit.

**LEARNING OBJECTIVES**
**STEPPING STONE**
Relate and make attachments to members of their group.

**EARLY LEARNING GOAL**
Work as part of a group or class, taking turns and sharing fairly, understanding that there needs to be agreed values and codes of behaviour for groups of people, including adults and children, to work together harmoniously. (PSED)

**GROUP SIZE**
Individuals; small or large groups.

**HOME LINKS**
Tell parents and carers about your activity and ask them to make sure their child chooses and brings in a suitable toy.

# Bedtime routine

**LEARNING
OBJECTIVES
STEPPING STONE**
Demonstrate a sense
of pride in own
achievement.

**EARLY LEARNING
GOAL**
Dress and undress
independently and
manage their own
personal hygiene.
(PSED)

**GROUP SIZE**
Small groups.

### What you need
Home corner arranged with bed, covers, dressing-up night clothes; storybooks;
alarm clock; children's own toothbrushes; toothpaste; hairbrush; comb.

### What to do
Say the rhyme with the children
and talk about their nightly bedtime
routines. Invite them to tell you in
turn what they do – how they put
on their pyjamas, brush their teeth
and so on.

Show a small group of children
the home corner and invite them
to play 'bedtime' together. Suggest
that one child gets ready for bed
while the other acts as the carer,
reminding the child to get changed
and brush their teeth! Provide a
tube of toothpaste and, with the
'carer', supervise the 'child' brushing
his or her teeth at your sink before
'bedtime'. Talk about the importance
of caring for our teeth and hair,
particularly at the beginning and
end of each day. Encourage the
children to independently try on the
dressing-up clothes, doing up
buttons and so on.

When the 'child' is ready for bed
suggest he or she climbs into bed
while the 'carer' sets the alarm clock
and then reads the 'child' a story.

### Support and extension
Pair younger children with an older child to lead the play in the home corner.
Invite older children to suggest other bedtime routines that they can act
out together.

**HOME LINKS**
Suggest that children
bring in their
favourite bedtime
storybooks from
home for you to read
them to the whole
group at story time.

### Further ideas
■ Make a list of all the things that are done at bedtime, such as bathing,
changing clothes, brushing teeth, saying 'good night' and reading a story.
■ Discuss the things that are usually done in the morning, such as having
breakfast, getting dressed, having a wash, and opening the curtains.
■ Create a picture display showing 'Things we do at bedtime' compared with
'Things we do when we get up'.

# Thought for the day

### What you need
Coloured pens and pencils; drawing paper; drafting paper.

### What to do
Say the rhyme together and tell the children that some people say a prayer at bedtime. Remind the children about prayers by talking about any they may have heard during recent assemblies or at their local church, mosque or other place of worship.

Explain that some prayers are to give thanks to God for things that have happened to us or to people around us. Be aware of the different religions of the children in your group and be sympathetic to the different interpretations of the word 'God' and to different styles of praying.

Ask the children to recall a personal experience or general observation which they can be for thankful for, and invite them to draft their own prayer giving thanks. Suggest that they begin by writing 'Thank you God for... a happy day/special friend/beautiful flowers and so on.

When they are happy with their prayer, encourage the children to copy it out carefully on a sheet of paper or draw a picture to represent their prayer if appropriate. Ask the children to explain their prayer to the other children.

### Support and extension
Let younger children work together in a small group and all contribute ideas towards one shared prayer. Scribe the words for them and then let them illustrate the sheet. Invite older children to write their individual prayers into a blank book to create a prayer book to share.

### Further ideas
■ Invite the children to read out their prayers during assemblies or group sharing times.
■ Display the children's prayers alongside their 'Thank you' paintings and drawings.
■ Visit a local church, mosque or other religious centre. Arrange for someone to talk to the children about prayer time or other important rituals.
■ Read out a prayer or meditation from a different religion at the beginning of each day.

**LEARNING OBJECTIVES**
**STEPPING STONE**
Have an awareness of and show interest and enjoyment in, cultural and religious differences.

**EARLY LEARNING GOAL**
Understand that people have different needs, views, cultures and beliefs, that need to be treated with respect. (PSED)

**GROUP SIZE**
Small groups.

**HOME LINKS**
Ask parents and carers from a range of religions to come in and talk to the children about how they pray.

# The land that I dreamed of...

**LEARNING OBJECTIVES**

**STEPPING STONE**
Use talk, actions and objects to recall and relive past experiences.

**EARLY LEARNING GOAL**
Use language to imagine and recreate roles and experiences. (CLL)

**GROUP SIZE**
Small groups.

### What you need
Card (size A4 and slightly smaller); paper (slightly smaller than A4); pens; pencils; hole punch; ribbon or wool; the story of *The Wizard Of Oz* by L Frank Baum (Puffin); *Alice in Wonderland* by Lewis Carroll (Puffin) or another book with a dream sequence about a fantasy land.

### What to do
Say the rhyme together and talk about sleeping. Ask the children if they can remember any dreams they have had. Read extracts from books which contain dream sequences about a fantasy land to the children.

Discuss the dream lands featured in the books you have read. Ask the children to talk about their favourite sequences from each book and to describe which one of these dream lands they would most like to visit. Ask: Where would you most like to go in your dreams? Why?

Next, provide each child with two sheets of card (one A4 and the other slightly smaller than A4). Help the children to make a cover for their story by securing the card together using a hole punch and ribbon or wool and to decorate it to resemble themselves asleep in bed.

Encourage each child to write and/or draw about an imaginary land that they would like to visit in their dreams. Pose questions to stimulate their ideas, such as: What would your fantasy land look like? Where would it be? Who would you meet there? What would you do there? Who would you take with you? How would you get there? How would you get home?

The children can then give their story a title. Finish by helping them to secure their writing into their decorated cover.

### Support and extension
Invite younger children to begin by drawing or painting a picture of a 'dreamland' which can be used to stimulate ideas. Scribe the words for the children or encourage emergent writing. Encourage older children to begin by devising a draft of their story. Some children may also enjoy planning their work into story chapters or organising it to show a traditional beginning, middle and end.

### Further ideas
■ Invite the children to paint a picture about their 'dreamland'
■ Encourage the children to share their stories by reading them aloud or displaying them in the book corner.
■ Make a large collage depicting the children's favourite scenes from one or more of the story books.

**HOME LINKS**
Encourage children to recall their dreams by keeping a notepad by their beds to write down words or draw pictures about their dreams.

# The teddy bears' pyjamas

## What you need
The photocopiable sheet 'Pyjama game' on page 72; adhesive; scissors; card; coloured pens and pencils; ten small teddies.

## Preparation
Make a copy of the photocopiable sheet for each child.

## What to do
Say the rhyme together and let the children use ten small teddies to act out the parts of 'Ten in a bed'.

Hand out copies of the photocopiable sheet and encourage the children to identify the five pairs of teddies with matching pyjamas and to colour each pair so that they are identical.

Talk about the different shapes and patterns on the teddies pyjamas. Ask them to identify the zigzags, checks, horizontal lines, wavy lines, spots and so on. Talk about how different shapes are repeated to make patterns. Talk about words and phrases that can be used to describe matching, such as 'the same as', 'pairs' and 'alike'.

Help the children to cut carefully along the dotted lines and to stick the ten teddies onto ten pieces of card. Invite the children to use their pack of cards to play matching and sorting games such as 'snap' and 'pairs'. Can they explain to you how to play the games?

## Support and extension
For younger children enlarge the photocopiable page to make the pictures twice as big and let a group of children help to make one set of cards to share during simple matching and sorting activities. Invite older children to create a dice using sticky labels and a wooden brick. Each side of the dice should show one of the five pyjama patterns, leaving one side of the dice blank. Encourage the children to use the dice with their set of cards to invent original sorting and matching games.

## Further ideas
■ Design a pair of pyjamas or night-dress.
■ Help the children to sew a simple night-shirt or pyjamas for their favourite doll or teddy.
■ Let the children paint a pattern onto paper or fabric.

**LEARNING OBJECTIVES**
**STEPPING STONE**
Match some shapes by recognising similarities and orientation.

**EARLY LEARNING GOAL**
Talk about, recognise and recreate simple patterns. (MD)

**GROUP SIZE**
Small groups.

**HOME LINKS**
Ask the children to look at their own pyjamas and night-dresses at home and to tell you what patterns they have.

# Where do animals sleep?

## What do you need
The photocopiable sheet 'Time to sleep' on page 73; a small pet such as a hamster, gerbil or fish (optional); information books with photographs of animals sleeping in or near their 'beds'.

## Preparation
Copy the sheet, one per child. If you do have a small pet which you can bring in safely, make sure there are no allergies among the children and observe the sensible safety precautions at all times. Let the children spend time observing the pet's behaviour when it eats, sleeps, plays and rests. Talk about where it sleeps and what type of bedding (if any) it uses.

## What to do
Hand out copies of the photocopiable sheet and use the pictures to stimulate the children's curiosity and discussion about where animals sleep. Invite the children to think about the differences between where they sleep themselves compared to these animals.

Encourage the children to identify the six animals and the six habitats and then to cut along the dotted lines and stick the animal pictures into the correct position.

Talk about the unusual sleeping habits of some animals, such as a bat hanging upside down, a fish in water, a rabbit underground or a bird setting on a perch or in a nest. Ask the children what features all animals need where they sleep (somewhere warm, dry and safe), and ask if they need the same things in their bed.

## Support and extension
Let younger children tell you about their own experiences or what they know about pets. Encourage older children to pose questions such as: Does a fish close its eyes when sleeping? Can a person fall asleep while standing up? Does a worm ever go to sleep? Let them use information books or CD-Roms to find out the answers.

## Further ideas
■ Create a 'fact file' containing all the information that they have found out.
■ Use a word processing package to write up information, then print off the children's work.
■ Paint or draw animals from firsthand observations. Provide a magnifying glass for detailed observation.

### LEARNING OBJECTIVES
**STEPPING STONE**
Examine objects and living things to find out more about them.

### EARLY LEARNING GOAL
Find out about, and identify, some features of living things, objects and events they observe. (KUW)

### GROUP SIZE
Individuals, small or large groups.

### HOME LINKS
Ask children who have pets at home to find out where their pets sleep and what bedding they need and to tell the rest of the group what they have found.

# A toy bed

## What you need
The children's own dolls or teddy (or selection to choose from); commercial construction kits such as LEGO, Mobilo or Duplo; craft material such as boxes, card, fabric, sponge, dowelling, string, braid, ribbon; scissors; adhesive; pens; paper; pictures of a variety of beds (four poster, bunk beds, single beds, cots, camp beds, air beds and hammocks).

## What to do
Show the children the pictures of the different beds and talk about the various designs. Let the children talk about their own beds at home. What do they like to do in bed as well as sleep? Do they read there, listen to story tapes or play with their toys?

Suggest that the children make a bed for their toys and encourage them to begin by making a few rough sketches, showing the type of bed that they would like to make. Encourage them to consider factors such as size and strength of the bed and how they can decorate and 'pad' it to make it look inviting and feel comfortable.

Using the construction kits and craft materials, allow the children a free choice to make their beds. Encourage them to describe the toy beds as they are making them, explaining what techniques and materials they have chosen and why.

## Support and extension
Younger children may prefer to go straight to making their beds, rearranging and adapting their ideas as they work. Encourage older children to consider the type of toy they have and to design a suitable bed, for example, a baby doll could have a cot or a pram and a toy dog could have a dog basket.

## Further ideas
■ Make accessories for the toy bed such as blankets, sheets, pillows, cushions and a cover.
■ Ask the children to write about how they made their toy bed and to list the materials they used.
■ Invite the children to construct a model cupboard, chair, table or wardrobe for their toy to use.

**LEARNING OBJECTIVES**
**STEPPING STONE**
Demonstrate increasing skill and control in the use of mark-making implements, blocks, construction sets and 'small world' activities.

**EARLY LEARNING GOAL**
Handle toys, objects, construction and malleable materials safely and with increasing control. (PD)

**GROUP SIZE**
Individuals or small groups.

**HOME LINKS**
Suggest to the children that they use any construction kits they have at home to make beds for some of their other toys.

# Making a pyjama case

### What you need

Plain fabric (night sky colours such as black, dark blue, purple); fabric paints (moon and star colours such as white, yellow, gold, silver); assorted objects that can be used to make star and moon shaped prints; trays lined with sponge; thick card (or cardboard); masking tape; scissors; pinking shears; needles; thread; thick ribbon or card.

### Preparation

Use pinking shears (to prevent fraying) to cut the fabric into rectangles of 30cm × 60cm. Use masking tape to secure the rectangle of fabric onto a sheet of thick card, or cardboard to keep the fabric flat and manageable during the printing stage.

### What to do

Talk about how we go to bed at night-time, and ask the children how the sky looks different at night compared to daytime. Can the children tell you what different colours and shapes they can see in the sky during these times?

Invite the children to use the star and moon-shaped objects to print their own sky-at-night scene onto their fabric. Let them change their own design using the range of shapes and colours provided. When complete, remove the masking tape and hang up to dry.

Show the children how to fold their piece of fabric in half and to use simple running stitch to sew two of the open sides together, leaving one opening at the top. Help them to tack a length of thick ribbon or cord approximately 10cm from the opening. When the ribbon is securely attached, it can be used to tie the bag together.

### Support and extension

Younger children may need one-to-one help during the sewing stage. Older children can decorate the pyjama cases with a simple appliqué design, by cutting out shapes from non-fraying fabric and sewing or gluing pieces onto the printed fabric. Suggest a design such as a night owl or a rocket in space.

### Further ideas

■ Make up a group sequence book or poster describing how the pyjama bags were made using the children's writing and drawings.
■ Invite the children to work together to create a night-time collage.
■ Find out about which animals come out at night.

**LEARNING OBJECTIVES**
**STEPPING STONE**
Manipulate materials to achieve a planned effect.

**EARLY LEARNING GOAL**
Handle tools, objects, construction and malleable materials safely and with increasing control. (PD)

**GROUP SIZE**
Individuals or small groups.

**HOME LINKS**
Ask parents and carers to supply items such as cotton reels, or cut up vegetables such as potatoes for their children to make prints using paint.

# Composing a lullaby tune

## What you need
A range of percussion instruments; the words and music to traditional lullabies such as 'Bye baby bunting' and 'Rock-a-bye baby'.

## What to do
Say the rhyme together then ask the children to tell you what they can do to help themselves fall asleep. Explain that lullabies are one way to help. Talk about why and when lullabies are usually sung (at bedtime to help babies and children to fall asleep). Discuss why lullabies are gentle tunes rather than loud, jerky noises. Sing the traditional lullabies with the children and invite them to use their instruments to accompany them while they sing.

Next, invite the children to use the instruments to experiment creating a range of different sounds. Can they make loud, quiet, fast, slow, jerky gentle, rousing and calming music?

Ask the children to identify which of the sounds would be most suitable for a lullaby (the quiet, gentle, calming sounds). Encourage independence from the children while they experiment, arranging some of these sounds together to create a new lullaby tune.

## Support and extension
Allow younger children time to try out and experiment with all the instruments individually. Invite older children to make up words for their new tune.

**LEARNING OBJECTIVES**
**STEPPING STONE**
Explore the different sounds of instruments.

**EARLY LEARNING GOAL**
Recognise and explore how sounds can be changed, sing simple songs from memory, recognise repeated sounds and sound patterns and match movements to music. (CD)

**GROUP SIZE**
Small groups.

## Further ideas
■ Use a cassette recorder to record the new tunes.
■ Invite the children to make their own percussion instruments for producing gentle sounds.
■ Listen to some music that may be new to the children such as music from other countries, classical, big band music, or music from other eras such as the 20s, 30s and 40s.

**HOME LINKS**
Ask parents and carers to allow their children to play some gentle music when they are in bed, to help them get to sleep.

# Milkshake bedtime drink

### What you need
**Ingredients**: a pint of milk; 100g of soft fresh fruit (strawberries, raspberries, banana) or tinned fruit (apricots, pineapple); chocolate flake; caster sugar; a scoop of vanilla ice cream (optional). Makes three drinks.
**Utensils**: a blender or hand whisk; fork; plastic bowl; ½ pint plastic tumblers; straws; aprons.

### Preparation
Ask the children to wash their hands and each put on a clean apron. Place the peeled and chopped fruit in a bowl and mash it with a fork. Check for any food allergies and intolerances.

### What to do
Tell the children that it is good to have a milky drink before we go to bed as it helps us to sleep. Explain that you are going to make a milkshake together.

Place the mashed fruit, milk, sugar and ice cream into a blender and mix for 30 seconds. If you do not have a blender, mix with a whisk or fork. Pour into two tumblers. Sprinkle flaked chocolate on top. Drink with a straw immediately.

Ask the children to recall the ingredients and sequence of events. Ask them: How many grams of fruit did you use? How did you mix the ingredients together? What did you do to the fruit first? How long did it take to fully mix the ingredients together?

### Support and extension
Prompt younger children in their recollection of the sequence of events. Invite older children to write or draw about their milkshake recipe.

### Further ideas
■ Encourage the children to wash up the utensils and clean the surfaces.
■ Invite the children to write or draw about their milkshake recipe.

**LEARNING OBJECTIVES**
**STEPPING STONE**
Show an interest in what they see, hear, smell, touch and feel.

**EARLY LEARNING GOAL**
Respond in a variety of ways to what they see, hear, smell, touch and feel. (CD)

**GROUP SIZE**
Three children at a time.

**HOME LINKS**
Suggest that parents and carers offer their children a milky drink before bedtime to help them sleep.

# Pat-a-cake

Introduce this traditional simple clapping rhyme to the children, inviting them to join in by clapping along rhythmically as you say the words. Explore the idea of a 'baker's man' with these activity ideas to extend the children's skills across all curriculum areas.

## A recipe for kindness

### What you need
A comfortable place to sit; sheet of A1 paper; pens and pencils.

### Preparation
Draw a large red heart on the sheet of paper.

### What to do

Ask the children to sit down on the carpet and encourage them to share their views and ideas about 'being kind', inviting them to talk about somebody who has been kind or caring towards them. Ask each child to recall something kind, helpful or loving which this person has done for them.

Tell the children that you are going to write a 'recipe for kindness' and explain that this is not a real recipe that they can follow in the kitchen. Refer back to the rhyme and explain to the children that all the items in the baker's shop need a recipe that includes all the different things needed to make the food. In this activity they are writing a 'recipe for kindness'.

Let the children take turns to write down their special memory inside the large heart (or scribe the words for them). When it is complete, add the caption 'A recipe for kindness', and mount it on the wall to create an eye-catching and thought-provoking display.

### Support and extension
Invite younger children to draw a picture of their special memory or a kind person to place inside the heart. Invite older children to draw or cut out a small heart of their own to write in. Help them to write the caption 'A recipe for love' on one side and to list all the ingredients that make someone loving on the other side. Thread all the hearts together to create a mobile.

### Further ideas
■ Write a thank you card or letter to someone who has been kind.
■ Make heart-shaped biscuits to share with friends and relatives.

---

**LEARNING OBJECTIVES**
**STEPPING STONE**
Begin to accept the needs of others, with support.

**EARLY LEARNING GOAL**
Understand what is right, what is wrong and why. (PSED)

**GROUP SIZE**
Small or large groups.

**HOME LINKS**
Suggest that parents and carers encourage their children to write letters of thanks when they receive gifts.

# What can we buy?

**LEARNING OBJECTIVES**
**STEPPING STONE**
Use writing as a means of recording and communicating.

**EARLY LEARNING GOAL**
Attempt writing for different purposes, using features of different forms such as lists, stories and instructions. (CLL)

**GROUP SIZE**
Whole group

### What you need
Table-cloth; modelling dough; card; crayons; paper plates; boxes; felt-tipped pen; pictures of bakery items (from magazines); bakery product packages.

### What to do
Ask the children to help you to set up a role-play bakery counter on a corner table. Invite the children to use the modelling dough to make different shaped loaves, buns, biscuits and cakes. Alternatively, use pieces of card and stick on pictures from magazines. Put the cloth on the table and arrange all of the items on paper plates and in boxes and display them on the counter with packaging from relevant actual food items.

Talk about some of the items you might find at the bakery counter such as: bun, roll, pie, custard tart, jam tart, doughnut, small loaf, large loaf, sliced loaf, crusty bun, soft roll, biscuit, sandwich, cheese straw, teacake, crumpet, waffle and pizza. Point out and focus on the sounds and letters that the children know or are learning.

Suggest that the children make labels for the items on display, asking them to help you write the name of each one on a separate piece of card. With the children, think up a price for each item and write that on the card as well. Put each card beside the relevant item on the counter.

Ask the children to make several short lists, using only three or four items on each, showing the items and their prices. Stand the lists up on the bakery counter or fasten them to the wall behind it.

Let the children play at matching the words from the lists with the words on the plates or by the boxes.

### Support and extension
With younger children, limit the number of items you have on the counter to just a few to begin with. Add more items, once they are familiar with the first few. Encourage older children to use the play money to pay for their items, and to work out the cost of what they're buying.

### Further ideas
■ Visit a local bakery counter with the children and buy one or two items.
■ Write a 'list poem' together about things you can buy at the bakery.
■ Play 'We went to the baker's and bought…' sitting in a circle and asking each child to add another item to the list.

**HOME LINKS**
Ask parents and carers to let their children help to make shopping lists at home and to check items off the list when they are at the shops together.

# Where is it?

## What you need
Paper; pencils; crayons or felt-tipped pens; black felt-tipped pen; pieces of card; small bag.

## Preparation
Make a set of flashcards with directional words on, using a black felt-tipped pen on pieces of card. The words can include 'over', 'under', 'through', 'across', 'inside', 'outside', 'before', 'after', 'round', 'down', 'up'. Put the words in a bag.

## What to do
Tell the children that you are going to tell them a story and they have to find out where the baker's shop in the story is. Give each child a piece of paper and a pencil and ask them to start by drawing a picture of a house in the one corner of their paper.

Begin the story by saying, 'Dad wanted to buy some bread. He had to get to the baker's shop. He went…' pause and pull one of the words from the bag and show it to the children. Help them to read it and tell you what might come next. For example, if the word is 'down' they might say 'down the path.' They then draw the path.

Pull out another word, it might be 'through' and the children might suggest 'through the woods'. They can then draw the woods. Continue the process until Dad has 'travelled' all the way from the house to the baker's shop. Let them draw the baker's shop at the end of the journey.

When the pictures are finished, ask the children to trace Dad's journey from beginning to end, by running their fingers over the page talking through what happened next each time.

Ask the children what would happen if you put all the words back in the bag and started again. Would you get the same journey?

## Support and extension
With younger children, restrict the words to provide a short and simple story. With older children, do the exercise again and find out how many different journeys the children can draw. When they have had a couple of successful attempts, let them try writing the words rather than drawing the pictures to tell the story.

## Further ideas
■ Draw a simple map of a journey which the children know and encourage them to verbalise it, using the place words.
■ Make another bag of words, this time with nouns such as 'bridge', 'underpass', 'steps', 'river', 'street', 'crossing' and repeat the activity to tell a story using your own directional instructions.
■ To encourage pencil control, let the children complete the photocopiable sheet 'Follow the paths' on page 74.

### LEARNING OBJECTIVES
**STEPPING STONE**
Begin to recognise some familiar words.

**EARLY LEARNING GOAL**
Retell narratives in the correct sequence, drawing on language patterns of stories. (CLL)

### GROUP SIZE
Four or five children.

### HOME LINKS
Suggest that parents and carers talk with their child about the route they take to your group, to encourage them to think about the sequence of their journey.

# Big cakes, small cakes

## What you need

Ingredients for salt dough (in proportions of two mugs plain flour/one mug of salt/dessertspoon of cooking oil, water); cool oven; powder paint; varnish; aprons; table covering.

## What to do

Make a batch of dough with the children by mixing together the dry ingredients and adding water, a little at a time.

Ask the children to put aprons on and cover the table. Give each child some dough and ask them to form and pat it into lots of cakes of varying sizes. Bake the cakes in a cool oven until they are hard and then let the children paint and decorate them. The cakes can be varnished when the paint is dry.

Place all the completed cakes together and ask the children to work as a group to sort them in to size order, beginning with the biggest. Start by asking them which one is biggest of all. Then ask: Which one is smallest? Which one is just a little bit bigger than the smallest? Pick up individual cakes. Ask, which are smaller than this one? Which are bigger than this one? Which is fatter than this one? Next let the children suggest other ways to sort them for example, beginning with the fattest or the thinnest, the heaviest or the lightest. Encourage them to use the appropriate vocabulary as they sort.

## Support and extension

With younger children, make sure that the cakes are obviously different sizes to make sorting easier. As older children make their cakes, give them instructions to make a small one, a tiny one a bit bigger, one a bit bigger than that, a big one, and a huge one.

## Further ideas

■ Teach measuring vocabulary by using the children themselves, their feet, their clothing, toys, the room and so on, as examples of relative size.
■ When the children have finished the sorting activities, ask them to display their cakes in order and label them small/smaller/smallest and so on.
■ Give each child a copy of the photocopiable sheet 'How many cakes?' on page 75 to practise simple counting and addition skills.

**LEARNING OBJECTIVES**
**STEPPING STONE**
Use size language such as 'big' and 'little'.

**EARLY LEARNING GOAL**
Use language such as 'greater', 'smaller', 'heavier' or 'lighter' to compare quantities. (MD)

**GROUP SIZE**
Up to six children.

**HOME LINKS**
Ask parents and carers to use size vocabulary with their children at home, asking them to get small plates ready for tea, or to put big spoons out to serve food.

# Baker's shop game

## What you need
Pens; pencils; glue; card; dice marked 1 to 6; 1p, 2p and 5p coins (real or play); a small plastic pot (a yoghurt pot); counters; the photocopiable sheet, 'Cakes for sale' on page 76.

## Preparation
Provide each child with a copy of the photocopiable sheet and invite them to write a price up to the value of 5p for each cake or biscuit. They can then colour the cakes, cut along the dotted lines and stick their pictures onto a sheet of card, arranging them in any pattern.

## What to do
Explain to the children how to play the baker's shop game, which is for up to four players. Each player has one counter and plenty of 1p, 2p and 5p coins. You will need a pot of extra change nearby.

All players begin by placing their counters on any one of the pictures on the game board. The first player then throws the dice and moves accordingly in any direction around the board. They must 'pay' for the cake they land on by placing the required amount of money into the money pot (this pot can also be used to collect change). If they do not have the exact change to buy the cake, they can exchange money in the money pot.

Play continues with the players taking turns to throw the dice and move around the board. The aim is for each player to buy all eight cakes.

Afterwards, ask the children to explain to you how they made their game. Ask: Which is the most expensive/cheapest cake on the board? Can they tell you all the rules for the game? Who is the winner? Why?

## Support and extension
Provide only 1p coins for younger children to use. For older children, provide more money to spend and use higher price tags. Let the children take it in turns to be a 'shopkeeper' by taking charge of the money pot and giving out change to the other players.

## Further ideas
■ Ask the children to make their own dice and counters.
■ Write out the rules for the game and let the children illustrate them.

**LEARNING OBJECTIVES**
**STEPPING STONE**
Count up to three or four objects by saying one number name for each item.

**EARLY LEARNING GOAL**
Use developing mathematical ideas and methods to solve practical problems. (MD)

**GROUP SIZE**
Small groups.

**HOME LINKS**
Ask parents and carers to play other games using dice and counters with their children at home.

# Bringing the bread

### What you need
Plenty of space.

**LEARNING OBJECTIVES**

**STEPPING STONE**
Begin to differentiate between past and present.

**EARLY LEARNING GOAL**
Find out about past and present events in their own lives, and in those of their families and other people they know. (KUW)

**GROUP SIZE**
Whole group.

### What to do
Start by talking about how bread is made, and where we get it from; most children will probably know the supermarket as the main source. Explain that not very long ago, bread used to be bought at the baker's shop or delivered by the baker. The baker would travel around in a van full of different kinds of bread and cakes. He would open up the van at the back, pile bread and cakes into a huge bread basket, and knock on the door to see what the customer wanted to buy.

Compare buying bread like this, to buying bread today. Talk about similarities and differences. Do you think the bread was the same? Was it wrapped in plastic packaging? Was it sliced? Was there much variety? What reasons can you give for your ideas? If you could choose, which would you have – delivery rounds or supermarkets? Why?

Put the children in small groups, some to be customers, some to be bakers. Let them improvise a role-play pretending that the baker is coming with the bread in the basket to see what the customer wants to buy.

After the improvisation, sit the children in a circle and begin, 'The baker brings the bread. He knocks at the door…' and the child next in the circle says '…and I ask for one (bun).' The next child says '…and I ask for one (bun), and two (cakes)…'. And so on, around the circle adding new items.

### Support and extension
Encourage younger children to play 'bakers' in the home corner. Show them the process of making the dough and cooking the bread, and then how to organise 'deliveries'. Get older children to sharpen up their improvisations until they can build them into little storylines or dramas that they can present to the rest of the group.

### Further ideas
■ Write list poems of 'The baker brings the bread…' game.
■ Take a trip to the local baker's or supermarket bakery for observation.
■ Record the trip by making 'We went to the baker's' information books.

**HOME LINKS**
Encourage the children to talk to their grandparents or great-grandparents to find out ways in which daily life has changed.

# What can you clap?

## What you need
Large space.

## What to do
Practise the 'Pat-a-cake' rhyme plenty of times so that the children have a good idea of clapping to the words and rhythm. Practise it several times with the children, once with ordinary palm-to-palm clapping, once clapping the rhythm on their knees, and once clapping hands with a partner.

Next, clap patterns for the children to follow, such as slow, slow, fast, fast, slow or fast, fast, fast, slow, slow. Start with more simple patterns to give the children confidence.

Clap the rhythms of different songs that the children already know, such as 'Here we go Round the Mulberry Bush', 'Ring-a-ring o' roses', 'Here we go Gathering Nuts in May' and 'The Hokey-cokey' and see if the children can guess which songs they are. Clap the songs with them using either palm-to-palm clapping, hand to knee clapping or clapping hands with a partner.

Ask the children how easy or difficult it is to guess a tune from the rhythm. Invite individual children to clap a song they know for the others to guess, or to clap a new pattern for everyone to follow.

## Support and extension
Give younger children plenty of time to try and follow the patterns that you clap. Keep the patterns simple and restrict them to hand clapping until they are confident with the pattern (it's harder to make a clapping noise with hand to knee and partner-clapping) For older children, do the clapping patterns more quickly in succession. You clap a pattern, they respond, you clap another pattern, they respond, and so on. Try not to leave any gaps.

## Further ideas
■ Clap out the children's names to help them to understand syllables.
■ Play some music and try to clap the rhythm of it after listening for a short while.
■ Play a game where clapping takes the place of some instruction. For example three fast claps mean stand up, two slow claps mean sit down, two fast claps, a beat and two more claps mean cross your legs.

**LEARNING OBJECTIVES**
**STEPPING STONE**
Respond to rhythm, music and story by means of gesture and movement.

**EARLY LEARNING GOAL**
Move with confidence, imagination and in safety. (PD)

**GROUP SIZE**
Whole group.

**HOME LINKS**
Invite parents and carers to teach their children any clapping games or rhymes that they remember from their own school days.

# Let's be bakers

**LEARNING OBJECTIVES**
**STEPPING STONE**
Experiment with different ways of moving.

**EARLY LEARNING GOAL**
Move with confidence, imagination and in safety. (PD)

**GROUP SIZE**
Whole group.

## What you need
Large space.

## What to do
Talk about the baker's shop and tell the children how bread is made. Explain that the baker mixes the ingredients to make the dough and then kneads it thoroughly, stretching and pulling the dough with firm fingers and patting it with the heel of the hand to introduce air. The dough has to be left to rise and double its size. The next step is to knock air bubbles out of the bread, briefly knead it again, divide the dough into shape, and leave it to 'prove', when it doubles in size again.

Tell the children to imagine they are bakers and to get into the shape of a traditional baker. First, they are mixing the ingredients with a wooden spoon, next they must knead the dough, stretching it, pulling, bashing it with the heel of their hands.

Now they can become the dough! Ask them to take their positions on the floor and feel themselves being pulled and stretched pummelled and turned over and over. Pretend to break the dough and mould it into shapes, they could become crescent shapes, bun shapes, or long, thin roll shapes. They should lie as still as they can then as slowly as possible puff themselves up as the dough rises. Ask them to start in a low, curled position, gradually stretching higher and wider, turning slowly on the spot.

Get the children to demonstrate their actions to the others. Who can show us how to be a baker? Who can show us how to pummel and pull the dough? Who can show us how to be stretched and pulled as far as we can?

## Support and extension
Encourage younger children to do follow-the-leader patterns of stretching and making shapes, asking them to copy each other. Ask older children to develop their skills as bakers: getting the bread out of the oven, tapping the bottom to see if it makes a hollow sound and is therefore cooked properly, piling the bread up on the bread basket or the shelves.

**HOME LINKS**
Ask the children to find out what different types of bread are eaten at home and to describe the different types and shapes to the other children.

## Further ideas
■ Find a simple recipe and make bread rolls with the children.
■ Ask the children to suggest as many cooking actions as they can: stirring, shaking, beating, patting into shape. Encourage the children to act them out, using their bodies to make different shapes.

# Name badges

## What you need
Small pieces of card; felt-tipped pens; sticky coloured paper; sticky paper; Sellotape; scissors.

## Preparation
Draw cake shapes on the cards. Ensure the children know what their initials are and how to write them.

## What to do
Remind the children of the rhyme. In the rhyme, the baker marks the cake with B for Baby. Tell the children they are going to make their own cake badge with their initials on.

Help the children to decorate their cakes with pieces of sticky coloured paper to represent icing, cherries and other decorations and then to mark the cakes with their initials using the felt-tipped pens. Talk about the letters as you help them write. What does B stand for? What does T say in your name, Tom? How do you do a T? Where do you start? Let's start at the top and come down, making a stick, then go back to the top and put another stick across and so on. They can then cut the cake out.

Fold the Sellotape over to make it double-sided and show the children how to fix their name badges to their clothes, their pencil cases, their books, or their bags.

## Support and extension
Younger children might find it easier to cut a straight or circular shape around the cake than to try to follow the edges of the cake. With a felt-tipped pen, draw a line around the outside for them to follow with the scissors. Let older children work out who the badges belong to by reading the letters.

## Further ideas
■ Make an alphabet frieze by drawing block letters of the alphabet and letting the children colour them in. Cut them out and ask the children to help you arrange them in alphabetical order and stick them to the wall with double-sided Sellotape.

■ Make your frieze more elaborate by sticking envelopes to it, one for each letter. Ask the children to cut out pictures of words that begin with that letter and put them in the right envelope.

**LEARNING OBJECTIVES**
**STEPPING STONE**
Make constructions, collages, paintings, drawings and dances.

**EARLY LEARNING GOAL**
Explore colour, texture, shape, form and space in two or three dimensions. (CD)

**GROUP SIZE**
Up to six children.

**HOME LINKS**
Suggest that parents and carers provide craft materials for their children to make cut and stick pictures at home.

# Fill up the counter

**LEARNING OBJECTIVES**
**STEPPING STONE**
Work creatively on a large or small scale.

**EARLY LEARNING GOAL**
Explore colour, texture, shape, form and space in two or three dimensions. (CD)

**GROUP SIZE**
Up to six children.

## What you need
Paper; card; paints; felt-tipped pens; crayons; coloured sticky paper; scissors; pictures of bakery items and packages from a bakery.

## Preparation
Have all the art materials organised in the centre of the table or space.

## What to do
Tell the children that they are going to make some bakery items themselves. Show them the pictures you have collected and the bakery items, and let them choose which item or items they want to make, and how they are going to make them.

Give them free choice for planning and making their items, helping and encouraging where necessary. Talk about what the children want to do. Let them describe what their item will look like. Ask them: how will you make it work? How will you show the cherry on top? How do you know how big to make it? How will you cut it out? How will you colour it? When the items are finished ask: is it how you wanted it? Can you think of a way to make it better? Can you make another one the same?

## Support and extension
Use sugar paper and card with younger children rather than painting paper, which tends to tear easily. Make sure they know exactly what they want to do before they begin. Encourage older children to make specific sets of items, for instance, six cherry Bakewell tarts and ten jam doughnuts.

## Further ideas
■ Make salt dough bakery items (see recipe on page 40)
■ Help the children to write clear labels for their items.
■ Make a montage of pictures cut from magazines and catalogues.
■ Organise the children in a role-play to buy and sell the bakery items.

**HOME LINKS**
Ask parents and carers to contribute pictures of bakery items or packages from the bakery for this activity.

# Old Mother Hubbard

Use this popular nursery rhyme as a good starting point to develop the children's sense of history and the past. The ideas will help them learn about the way we used to live, how we cooked and looked after our homes, all about shopping and how to look after their pets.

## Would you like some?

### What you need
A comfortable place to sit; small sweets (one each); writing materials; one sheet of A3 paper; a sheet of A4 paper for each child.

### Preparation
Cut each piece of A4 paper into the shape of a pair of hands. Cut the A3 paper into a large pair of hands and label one hand 'caring' and one hand 'sharing'.

### What to do
Begin by choosing one child to share out some sweets among the other children. Discuss with the children how they used their hands to perform this task, in the same way as Old Mother Hubbard used her hands to prepare and share her food with the dog.

Display the large pair of hands (A3 sheet) and ask the children to share their ideas on other tasks they can do with their hands. Develop the discussion into ways in which our hands can be used to help each other by sharing and caring, for example, sharing our toys and helping our parents.

Encourage the children in turn to describe a time when they have shared something with a friend. Record these ideas on the large 'sharing hand'. Repeat, this time discussing how children can care for each other and animals. Record these contributions in the same way on the 'caring hand'. Encourage the children to contribute when appropriate, take turns and respect others' opinions and beliefs.

Once this is completed, give each child a pair of 'sharing' and 'caring' hands (cut from the A4 sheets) and ask them to record their own particular memory on their own 'hand' sheets.

### Support and extension
Invite younger children to draw a picture of a sharing time and ask an adult to scribe the event on their behalf. Encourage older children to record their caring and sharing memories by writing on their 'hands' using sentences.

### Further ideas
■ Role-play some of the events, extracting feelings from the children.
■ Create a peacock display from handprints. Add a hand each time the children do something to share during the day.

---

**LEARNING OBJECTIVES**
**STEPPING STONE**
Relate and make attachments to members of their group.

**EARLY LEARNING GOAL**
Work as part of a group or class, taking turns and sharing fairly, understanding that there needs to be agreed values and codes of behaviour for groups of people, including adults and children, to work together harmoniously. (PSED)

**GROUP SIZE**
Small or large groups.

**HOME LINKS**
Suggest that the children help around the house whenever they can such as putting away their toys and keeping their bedrooms tidy. Talk about helping parents and carers around the home.

# Food, glorious food

## What you need
Shopping bags; outdoor clothes; overalls for shop workers.

## Preparation
Divide the children into three groups to represent shoppers, shop workers (including till operator and shelf stacker) and family members. Discuss the different tasks carried out by all the members of each group so that the children are clear about the different roles.

## What to do
Explain that as Old Mother Hubbard needed to go shopping to fill her shelves, so the children are going to do the same.

Tell the children that each member of each group is going to have a particular task to do, in order that food can be bought and cooked. Encourage the children to cooperate and work together in their groups and try to ensure that all the children are involved in the conversations.

Brief each group:

**Shoppers** – the cupboards are empty and they need to be filled. The shoppers' task is to decide what food is to be bought. What is your favourite food? Do you sell it in packets or tins? How much do you need to buy?

**Shop workers** – the shelves need to be stacked and customers need to be served. The shop workers' job is to talk with their group and decide which items need restocking, how to use the till and what to say to customers. Which product is the most popular? Which foods would you stack next to each other? What buttons on the till do you need to press?

**Family members** – they have returned home and want to know what they will have to eat and how long the meal will take to prepare. They should have a chat around the dinner table. What would you like to eat? What have you done today? What are you going to do later?

Let the three groups work separately and then together to develop their role-play. Once they have had sufficient time to work together and develop their ideas the three groups can re-enact their whole section in sequence to show the order of events.

## Support and extension
With younger children, choose one aspect of the role-play and lead the conversation, giving helpful hints in order to move the children forward. Extend the activity by using the role-play area to develop the idea after the initial input. Encourage older children to make a written record of some aspect of their task.

## Further ideas
■ Develop simple scripts and use these within the role-play area; turn it into a recording or film studio!
■ Introduce further characters and props to extend the dramatisation or create new scenes.
■ Dramatise other familiar stories.

**LEARNING OBJECTIVES**
**STEPPING STONE**
Link statements and stick to a main theme or intention.

**EARLY LEARNING GOAL**
Speak clearly and audibly with confidence and control and show awareness of the listener, for example by their use of conventions such as greetings, 'please' and 'thank you'. (CLL)

**GROUP SIZE**
Small groups.

**HOME LINKS**
Encourage parents and carers to involve their children in tasks at home by helping to write shopping lists, visiting the shops together and planning meals.

# Going to the shops

## What you need
Sheet of A3 paper; sheet of A4 paper for each child; pencils; crayons; coloured pencils; empty box; one item of food.

## Preparation
Turn the empty box into a cupboard shape with opening doors. Fold the A4 and A3 paper into the shape of a cupboard. Place an item of food inside the cardboard box 'cupboard'.

## What to do
Place the cardboard 'cupboard' on the floor near to the children. Choose a child to represent Old Mother Hubbard and explain that she has fed the dog and now she is going to have her dinner. Send the child to open the cupboard for some food, when the child opens the cupboard she finds only one item of food. Explain that she must go shopping for some more food.

Ask the children in turn what they would like to buy from the shops. They can each reply using the phrase, 'Old Mother Hubbard needs some…'. Suggest that there is too much shopping to remember and that you need to write a list. Introduce the large A3 'paper cupboard' and write or draw on it what the children would choose to buy.

Now give each child their own 'paper cupboards' (folded A4 sheets) to fill them with shopping lists. Let them choose some items and ask them to draw a picture of each food item or write the words.

Talk with the children about when they go shopping. Ask: Who do you go with? Do you take a shopping list? Which shops do you go to? How do you get there?

## Support and extension
With younger children scribe the words or encourage the children to create their own pictorial shopping list. Encourage older children to write shopping lists either working independently or arranging the lists in alphabetical order. When reciting 'Old Mother Hubbard buys.' Ask them to memorise and sequence the previous foods suggested by the other children (as in 'I went on holiday and I took…').

## Further ideas
■ Set up a shop in the role-play area.
■ Make an alphabet book – think of a food for each letter.
■ Make shopping bags from coloured paper, wrapping paper or card and add fasteners and a handle (Sellotape, split pins, glue, stapler, ribbon, string).

**LEARNING OBJECTIVES**
**STEPPING STONE**
Use writing as a means of recording and communicating.

**EARLY LEARNING GOAL**
Attempt writing for different purpose, using features of different forms such as lists, stories and instructions. (CLL)

**GROUP SIZE**
Small groups.

**HOME LINKS**
Encourage the children to role-play shopping at home, making their own lists and acting out shopping with parents, carers and siblings.

# Whose dinner is it?

**LEARNING
OBJECTIVES
STEPPING STONE**
Examine objects
and living things to
find out more about
them.

**EARLY LEARNING
GOAL**
Find out about,
and identify, some
features of living
things, objects and
events they observe.
(KUW)

**GROUP SIZE**
Small groups.

### What you need
Pictures of a selection of animals (ducks, birds, squirrels, lions, cows and lambs); pictures of what these animals eat (worms, apples/nuts, pieces of meat, grass and milk); ribbons or laces; paper plates; Blu-tack.

### Preparation
Place the pictures of food on paper plates. Make labels for the food and animals. Place Blu-Tack at each end of the ribbons or laces.

### What to do
Remind the children that in the rhyme, Old Mother Hubbard had to feed her dog. Ask the children to think about what animals eat.

Next, look at each animal picture individually and encourage the children to name them in turn, place the relevant label by each animal as it is named. Encourage the children to describe the animals in detail and highlight the differences between them. Pay particular attention to the shapes of the animals' mouths, describing the size and shape as well as the action used by the particular animals to feed. Introduce some descriptive eating words such as chewing, gnawing, sucking, chomping and grinding. Discuss whether these animals are living things and ask how we know this (they need food to survive, breathe and move).

Pass around the plates of food pictures for the children to examine and ask the children to describe them by texture, shape and so on. When they have described and successfully named each food item, label them appropriately.

Encourage the children to guess which plate of food each animal would like to eat, and ask them why they think this. Use the ribbon/laces to link each animal to the correct plate of food.

### Support and extension
With younger children, focus the activity around two more familiar animals such as cats and dogs, and follow this up with practical experiences using small-world play. For older children, provide paper and drawing materials and ask them to predict the food which each animal may eat before the examples of food are revealed. Discuss in greater detail the characteristics of living things – moving, feeding, growing, using senses and reproducing.

**HOME LINKS**
Encourage children
to help care for any
pets they may have
at home, helping
to feed and groom
them.

### Further ideas
■ Give the children copies of the photocopiable sheet, 'What do we eat?' on page 77 and ask them to cut out all the pictures and match up the animals with their food.
■ Talk about and investigate animals' habitats.
■ Tell the children animal stories and some of Aesop's tales, for example, *The Fox and the Stork*.

# How we used to cook

## What you need
Household equipment from role-play area, such as washing-machine, cooker, iron (with string for cord), ironing board, pans, plates, washing-powder, table and chairs and so on; large box; bucket; red tissue paper; cardboard; blanket; round tub; pole; soap.

## Preparation
Position the table and chairs and set up an old-fashioned kitchen to one side and the modern one to the other.

**Old-fashioned kitchen:** make a kitchen range from a cardboard box with black circles and rectangles stuck on top to represent hot plates; place red tissue paper in the bucket and place in front of the box, to represent the hot coals; make an iron using cardboard, stand this next to the bucket; use the tub and pole to represent a dolly peg and wash tub, and place these next to the range; place a blanket on the table as an ironing board.

**Modern kitchen:** place the washing machine, cooker, ironing board and iron on one side of the table and chairs.

## What to do
Discuss with the children the type of chores undertaken in our kitchens today. Ask each child in turn to perform one task in the 'modern kitchen'. Take each task in turn, and encourage the child to describe how it is performed, stressing factors such as: using electricity or gas; switching things on and off.

Explain to the children that this is how chores are performed now, and ask them to think about how they were undertaken when their grandparents or great-grandparents were little. Use the old-fashioned kitchen to prompt the children, and when they suggest a task, invite them to re-enact it in the old-fashioned kitchen. Help them by describing the tasks in detail for example: long ago, there was no electricity or gas, so people had to use coals (bucket of tissue, to be placed inside the cardboard box to act as fire); long ago, to heat the iron, people had to put it onto the range, and they used a blanket on the table as an ironing board;.

Draw the children's attention to the comparisons and differences as the modern day and old-fashioned tasks are performed in each kitchen. Discuss which kitchen would be the hardest/easiest to work in and why. Talk about which kitchen the children would prefer to work in. Discuss any further aspects that can be compared, such as lights/candles, toaster/toasting fork.

## Support and extension
Let younger children role-play using the modern kitchen and the old-fashioned kitchen and highlight just one or two tasks for comparison. Ask older children to write or draw an account, 'A day in the life of my great-grandparents'.

## Further idea
■ Look at similarities and differences in other aspects of the home, such as bathrooms or sitting rooms.

---

**LEARNING OBJECTIVES**
**STEPPING STONE**
Show interest in the lives of people familiar to them.

**EARLY LEARNING GOAL**
Find out about past and present events in their own lives, and in those of their families and other people they know. (KUW)

**GROUP SIZE**
Small groups.

**HOME LINKS**
Invite a grandparent or great-grandparent to come in and talk to the children about what things were like when they were growing up.

# Stop and shop

**LEARNING OBJECTIVES**
**STEPPING STONE**
Sort objects by one function.

**EARLY LEARNING GOAL**
Look closely at similarities, differences, patterns and change. (KUW)

**GROUP SIZE**
Small groups.

### What you need
Fruit; cake; sweets; the photocopiable sheet 'Find the shop' on page 78; writing and colouring materials; three shoe boxes.

### Preparation
Label the three boxes 'shop' and put a mixture of fruit, cakes and sweets in each of the boxes. Copy the photocopiable sheet for each child.

### What to do
Place the three boxes of food on the floor near to the children. Point out that someone has mixed the food up in the shops. Encourage the children to try and sort the food into the correct shops.

Choose one child to sort the food in front of the shops, and another to explain why the food is sorted in that way,

Ask the children which shops they would buy these items from. Then label the shops, both pictorially and in writing, acting upon the children's advice. Now choose a child to place the items of food in the correct boxes, using the labels as a guide.

Talk about different types of shops. Discuss what is sold in supermarkets. What types of foods are put together on the shelves? How big is your supermarket? What can you find in the fridges? Why do you have to queue up in supermarkets? Do you think smaller shops are better than supermarkets?

Introduce the photocopiable sheet to the children and ask them to name the shops and the foods they could buy there. Ask them to match the foods to the correct shops, and colour them in.

### Support and extension
Give younger children the opportunity to sort the foods practically into the shoebox 'shops'. Ask older children to label some of their favourite foods.

### Further ideas
■ Introduce another shop box and discuss what food may be found there.
■ Talk about where different foods come from, such as apples from trees.
■ Consider what other local buildings are used for.

**HOME LINKS**
Ask parents and carer to let their children help to put food away after a food shop at home, thinking about what goes in the fridge and what in the cupboard.

# Food shapes

## What you need
Plenty of space.

## Preparation
Make sure children understand words such as *long, round, fat, thin, twisting,*. It will help if they are familiar with the game 'Simon Says'.

## What to do
Ask the children to each find a space where they can swing their arms around wide enough not to hit anybody else. Tell the children that they are going to be thinking about what shape different foods are and trying to copy those shapes. Talk about the different shapes and movements that the children can make by moving their bodies. Ask them to suggest some new words that you can incorporate into the game – twisty, pointed, curvy, wobbly, straight or frozen, for example.

Explain how to play the game: the leader calls out 'food can be round as a pea' and all the children must make themselves round. The leader calls out 'food can be as thin as a bean', and all the children must try to make themselves thin. The leader may say 'food can curl like a sausage', and the children do so. But if the leader says, 'curl like a sausage', without using the magic word 'food', then any child that makes the movement is 'out'.

## Support and extension
Start younger children off sitting in one space where they can easily make shapes and move their arms and legs without bumping into anyone else. For older children, try to speed up their interpretation and responses by giving the instructions faster, and find ways of introducing new movement words, such as 'leap', 'squat', 'rock'.

## Further ideas
■ Look for shapes in your environment so that you can reinforce the ideas of 'square', 'triangle', 'circle' and 'oblong' whenever possible.
■ Play 'Follow my leader' with the first child in the line deciding on a shape and way of moving, and the rest of the children imitating. The leader goes to the back of the line, and then the second child has a go.

### LEARNING OBJECTIVES
**STEPPING STONE**
Demonstrate the control necessary to hold a shape or fixed position.

**EARLY LEARNING GOAL**
Move with control and coordination. (PD)

### GROUP SIZE
Whole group.

### HOME LINKS
Ask parents and carers to provide regular opportunities for their children to use space, either by encouraging them to run around in an outdoors area or by taking them to swim or gym groups.

# I'm hungry!

## LEARNING OBJECTIVES
**STEPPING STONE**
Experiment to create different textures.

**EARLY LEARNING GOAL**
Explore colour, texture,, shape, form and space in two or three dimensions. (CD)

## GROUP SIZE
Small groups.

## What you need
Salt dough (see recipe on page 40); paper; card; sponge; small paper plates; aprons; polystyrene pieces; writing and colouring materials; paint; tissue paper; PVA glue; scissors and modelling tools (cutters, rollers).

## Preparation
Cover the work surface and display the range of materials in front of the children. Give each child a small paper plate and an apron.

## What to do
Explain that Old Mother Hubbard places the dog's food in a bowl, but we eat our food from a plate. Discuss with the children what their favourite foods are. Ask them to describe what the foods look like, what shape they are and how many of each thing they have on their plates.

Explain to the children that they are going to make a plate of their favourite food using some of the resources available. Make up an example plate of food, discussing with the children the appropriateness of the different materials for each food item. For example, you can use scrunched tissue paper for peas, cut out pieces of sponge for chips, and salt dough for eggs and sausage. Talk about the textures and how appropriate the materials are. Develop the children's vocabulary by using describing words such as spongy, springy, smooth and stretchy.

Now let the children select their materials and make up their chosen food items. As they work, ask questions such as: how could you make the sausages bigger? Once they have finished their food items and stuck them onto the plate, encourage them to paint or colour the food appropriately.

To finish and preserve the plates of food, carefully apply a thin layer of PVA adhesive as varnish.

## Support and extension
Let younger children fully explore the salt dough, encourage them to use rollers, cutters and shapes to improve their fine motor skills. Challenge older children to draft out their designs on pieces of paper, highlighting the materials needed and what they expect the finished plate of food to look like. The children can choose what they view as the most appropriate design before making their plate of food. Once their plate of food is finished, they should evaluate their product.

## HOME LINKS
Encourage the children to think about their favourite meals at home and to tell the rest of the group about them. Invite children from a range of cultures to contribute ideas for meals to make.

## Further ideas
■ Use self-drying clay or salt dough in order to make more durable plates of food.
■ Design and make labels, menus and price tags for the plates of food.
■ Set up a role-play restaurant or café for children to act out being the chef, waiters/waitresses and customers.
■ Play 'I went to the restaurant and I ate…'.

# Woof woof, miaow miaow

## What you need
Selection of animal pictures.

## Preparation
If possible, take the children to visit a pet shop or farm to observe animals in their own environment. Repeat the rhyme to the children and make up new verses introducing new animals.

## What to do
Encourage the children to gently tap their knees, and discuss whether the sound made is loud or quiet. Next, invite the children individually to experiment making other loud and quiet sounds.

Ask the children to make the sound of a mouse, and discuss whether a mouse's squeak is a high or low sound. Encourage the children to experiment making other high and low sounds.

Repeat this process each time, using a different animal sound to emphasise the various aspects: long or short, high or low, loud or quiet.

Now introduce the animal pictures and discuss the various sounds made. For example, show a picture of a cat and say 'The child says "miaow"', and ask the children to identify it as a high, long, quiet sound.

Discuss any relationship that exists between the size of the animal and the noises made. Can an elephant make a high sound? Is a mouse-sound long? Can you make a low sound? If you are little, is your voice squeaky? What noise would a hippopotamus make?

Once they have all had a turn and discussed the different sounds, choose a child to make a given animal sound, using one of the above elements. For example, ask a child to make an animal sound that is high ('tweet') or loud ('woof').

## Support and extension
Use a recording of actual animal sounds to help younger children determine the differences between a loud and quiet sound and a high and low sound. With older children develop the activity further by challenging them to work in pairs and make an animal sound using two or three of the elements. For example, 'moo' – a low, long and loud sound.

## Further ideas
■ Find out what sounds you can make using things in your group setting, such as banging blocks.
■ Sing 'How much is that doggy in the window?', changing the verses appropriately to include different animals.
■ Use percussion instruments and listen for different elements of sound.

**LEARNING
OBJECTIVES**
**STEPPING STONE**
Explore and learn
how sounds can be
changed.

**EARLY LEARNING
GOAL**
Recognise and
explore how sounds
can be changed, sing
simple songs from
memory, recognise
repeated sounds and
sound patterns and
match movements to
music. (CD)

**GROUP SIZE**
Whole group.

**HOME LINKS**
Ask parents and
carers to join you to
make a visit to a pet
shop or farm to see
and hear the animals.

# Look in the cupboard

**LEARNING
OBJECTIVES
STEPPING STONE**
Understand that
different media can
be combined.

**EARLY LEARNING
GOAL**
Explore colour,
texture, shape, form
and space in two or
three dimensions.
(CD)

**GROUP SIZE**
Whole group in
smaller groups.

### What you need
Display board or space; coloured paints; chalk; PVA glue; paper; shiny paper; tissue paper; brushes; aprons; table covering; pieces of net, wool, fur fabric; old combs or nailbrushes.

### Preparation
Cover the tables and divide the display board in half.

### What to do
Make a large display by drawing the outline of a cupboard on the left-hand side of your display board. Ask the children to paint the cupboard using brown paint mixed with PVA glue. While the paint is still wet, show them how to drag a nailbrush or comb through the paint to give the effect of wood grain. Stick shiny paper on the cupboard to represent handles.

Ask some children to draw a dog and stick on wool or fur fabric, to represent the fur. Make a bone shape out of paper to stick in a thought bubble.

Make Old Mother Hubbard by drawing an old woman outline, and use pieces of fabric for the dress and apron. Stick on wool for her hair and net for the mob cap. Use scrunched-up tissue paper for her features, and chalk in the eyes, mouth and eyebrows.

Repeat the above process on the other side of the board. This time leave the cupboard open, and make the old woman and dog look sad. Add an empty bowl for the dog. Attach a copy of the nursery rhyme to the display.

Brown paint
+ p.v.a glue/
wood grain
effect.

Paper bone.

Wool or fur
fabric.

Are you hungry?

Look in the cupboard.

Old Mother Hubbard

Net cap.

Wool.

Stuck on fabric.

But when

Empty cupboard.

dog

### Support and extension
Let younger children explore the materials and take part in sticking them on to shapes drawn by an adult. Ask older children to explain their choice of fabrics to the group, asking them why they have used wool for the dog and what the lines in the paint represent.

**HOME LINKS**
When the wall
display is complete
invite parents and
carers in to see the
work the children
have been doing on
the nursery rhyme.

### Further ideas
■ Make similar displays for other favourite nursery rhymes.
■ Ask the children to help you prepare displays on your current topic.

**10-MINUTE IDEAS: Nursery rhymes**

# The Wheels on the Bus

This popular and simple rhyme is ideal for topic work on transport, but can also be extended by changing the song words to fit any other early years theme. It offers opportunities to find out about people who help us and introduces some early road safety ideas.

## Signs for safety

### What you need
An outside observation point.

### What to do
Talk to the children about how roads are busy and what road accidents are, how they happen, and how they can be avoided.

Ask the children about how they come to and go home from your group. Who collects you? Is there a lollipop person? How do you know when it is safe to cross the road? Make sure they know and understand the Green Cross Code. Stress that children under eight years old should never cross a road unaccompanied.

Organise the children to go to the most appropriate point to observe the traffic passing by, and together look for:
- gates to stop the children running out into the road;
- signs outside the school or nursery, to slow the traffic down;
- road markings, to stop traffic parking where children might be crossing;
- traffic passing the school – it should be driving slowly;
- any provision for crossing, pelican crossing or lollipop person.

### Support and extension
Impress on younger children that they must look and listen for traffic when they cross roads with their parent or carer. Ask older children how many road signs they know. Ask them to look out for and remind each other of the signs. Can they draw and describe the signs to the rest of the group?

### Further ideas
- Make a large Green Cross Code poster; drill the children on learning it.
- Make a frieze to show the children coming to your group and crossing safely.
- Draw and label pictures of people who help the children to cross roads safely.

**LEARNING OBJECTIVES**
**STEPPING STONE**
Show care and concern for self.

**EARLY LEARNING GOAL**
Have a developing awareness of their own needs, views and feelings and be sensitive to the needs, views and feelings of others. (PSED)

**GROUP SIZE**
Five or six.

**HOME LINKS**
Ask parents and carers to talk about traffic awareness and road safety with their children. Stress to parents and carers that children under the age of eight should not cross roads unaccompanied.

# I'm on the bus

**LEARNING OBJECTIVES**

**STEPPING STONE**
Use talk, actions and objects to recall and relive past experiences.

**EARLY LEARNING GOAL**
Use language to imagine and recreate roles and experiences. (CLL)

**GROUP SIZE**
Any size.

## What you need
A comfortable space.

## Preparation
It would be useful (though not essential) to take the group on a bus journey beforehand.

## What to do
Sit the children in a circle and talk about different types of journeys – on foot, by car, by bus and so on. Focus on travelling by bus, some children may never have been on a bus at all, whereas, to many, it's a regular adventure. Let any children who travel on buses regularly tell the others about their experiences.

Next, encourage the children to all imagine they are on a bus and to think about what they can see, both inside and outside the bus. Ask them to choose a place where they could go on an imaginary bus trip. Ideally, make it somewhere the children all know, so that they have a good idea of the journey the bus might take and what they might pass on the way. If you have all been on a bus together, use that shared experience for the basis of the game.

Ask one child to begin, 'I'm going on the bus (to town). I can see (the library)'. The next child must repeat 'I'm going on a bus (to town). I can see (the library) and (the park)' expanding the list. The game then continues around the circle. Each child must repeat the list and add something extra.

Ask the children to concentrate, first on things inside the bus, then on things outside the bus. Keep the game going for as long as the children can manage to remember the list.

## Support and extension
With younger children, be ready to give clues to any child who has a problem, remembering their list and encourage the other children to help by finding, or pointing out, objects in your room. Make it more of a challenge for older children by choosing a place to go, but don't tell them where it is (town). Give clues by 'seeing' things beginning with the same letter or sound (toyshop, train) and see if they can guess the location.

**HOME LINKS**
Encourage parents and carers to take their children on a bus trip to the shops or the park to provide a new experience.

## Further ideas
■ Make a big storybook together in the shape of a bus.
■ Make a collection of toys with wheels.
■ Use the photocopiable sheet 'Who's on the bus?' on page 79 to develop the children's vocabulary and to aid their memories.

# How many wheels?

## What you need
Card; transport templates; felt-tipped pen; scissors; adhesive.

## Preparation
Cut out car, bicycle, bus and lorry shapes from the card. These can be very simple but make sure you provide a mixture of vehicles, some with two wheels, some four and some six or more. Cut out sets of card wheels in different sizes. Prepare an A4 sheet of paper, rule a line down the centre and write: 'How many wheels?' at the top of the column and 'How many vehicles?' at the top of the other and copy one for each child.

## What to do
Introduce the word 'vehicles' to the children and ask them which ones they know. Do all vehicles have wheels? Which vehicle has the most wheels? Which has the least? How many vehicles have you got at home? How many wheels do they have?

Give each child an assortment of card vehicles, the prepared sheet and a pencil. Place the wheels in sets according to size in the centre of the table. Let the children each choose a vehicle on which they can fix wheels. How many wheels will each vehicle need? Which size wheels? The children must take their wheels carefully, counting to make sure they have the right number. When they have the correct number they can stick the wheels to their vehicle. Show them that a bicycle will have two wheels and a car will have four, two each side of the card.

Help the children to glue their wheels onto their vehicles. Ask them to write the number of wheels for that vehicle in the first column and write '1' in the second column for the number of vehicles. They should draw a picture in this column to show whether it is a bike, car or truck. They can choose to colour the vehicles before or after the counting activity.

## Support and extension
With younger children, keep to low numbers and help them to add up the number of vehicles they have at the end. First, add up the number of vehicles column. Then add up the actual vehicles to which they have stuck wheels. Do they match? Ask older children to count their wheels out in pairs or twos. Help them to add up both columns and their vehicles; do the numbers match? How many wheels do they think they have used altogether? Do the numbers tally with the wheels on the vehicles?

## Further ideas
■ Learn some number rhymes such as, 'One potato, two potato'.
■ Make a hopscotch game with big sheets of card with numbers on them. Show the children how to play.
■ Give the children copies of the photocopiable sheet 'Match the wheels' on page 80 to develop observation skills.

---

**LEARNING OBJECTIVES**

**STEPPING STONE**
Count up to three or four objects by saying one number name for each item.

**EARLY LEARNING GOAL**
Count reliably up to 10 everyday objects. (MD)

**GROUP SIZE**
Three or four.

**HOME LINKS**
Ask the children to sort their toys at home to see which have wheels, finding as many different vehicles as possible. Let them talk about what they have found at circle time.

# Circles everywhere

### What you need
Nursery setting with equipment
and resources.

### What to do
Talk about the rhyme and how
the wheels on the bus are round.
Explain that we call the round
shape a circle and introduce the
children to some circle games, such
as 'Ring a Ring o' Roses', and 'I Sent
a Letter to my Love'.

Why do the children think
wheels need to be round? Have
you seen wheels another shape?
Would wheels work if they were
another shape? Why not?

Sit the children in a circle on
the floor and invite them, one-by-
one, to leave the group to find
something in the room that is a
circle. They can bring small objects
back to the group, or point to
things that aren't moveable. Run
your finger round the edge of
all the circles to show them how
the circles go round without a
beginning and without an end.

Go round the sitting circle again and ask each child to think of something
they know that has a circle (mug, cup, saucer, plate, tin of food and so on).

### Support and extension
Help younger children to notice the circles they are playing with, for example,
when they are playing in a sand pit or in the water tray, help them to notice
the circles on yoghurt pots, buckets or jugs. Instead of bringing their objects
to the sitting circle, invite older children to draw their ideas and if possible,
label them. They can show then show the pictures, explaining to the group
what their objects are and where they can see the circles.

### Further ideas
■ Draw a large chalk circle and ask the children to tiptoe, hop or skip around
its edges. Do the same with a figure 8.
■ Make a circle caterpillar by giving each child a paper plate or something to
draw round and cut out, and overlap the circles in a long wiggly line on the
wall, making a face at one end and putting two feet on each circle.

**LEARNING
OBJECTIVES
STEPPING STONE**
Match some shapes
by recognising
similarities and
orientation.

**EARLY LEARNING
GOAL**
Use language such
as 'circle' or 'bigger'
to describe the shape
and size of solids and
flat shapes. (MD)

**GROUP SIZE**
Whole group.

**HOME LINKS**
Suggest that parents
and carer cut circles
in potatoes and show
their children how to
make potato prints
with paint.

# Where shall we go?

## What you need
Large sheet of paper; felt-tipped pens.

## Preparation
Ask the children to decide on a location for a pretend trip on a bus. They can suggest somewhere real (encourage them to make up a fantasy name for it so they don't get confused when they're planning their route), or ask them to create their 'own' place. Make a simple drawing, marking out shaped blocks or spaces to show the route.

## What to do
Draw your chosen destination on the top or bottom right-hand corner of the sheet of paper and label it. Tell the children you are going to start the imaginary journey from 'home' in the diagonally opposite corner. Draw 'home' and label it. Explain that you now have to fill in all the rest of the paper in order to make your map.

What kind of things would they like on the map? Where should these things go? Help the children to decide and give them clues, for example, 'Do we need a school?', 'Do we need some shops?', 'Shall we have a train station?', 'Shall we have a river?'. Add some new things on the map that the children may not be familiar with, and include some road signs. Help the children to use as many place and direction words as possible, for example, over, through, left, behind and so on.

When you have drawn all the places on the map, concentrate on drawing in the bus route. Mark the bus route in a different colour and make it as twisty as possible to incorporate all the different places on the map.

Talk through the route you have made and let the children identify all the things they would see.

## Support and extension
With younger children, keep the plan quite simple and label everything with clues that will help them. For instance, although you may draw a bubble shape for wood, write the word 'wood' in it and draw a tree. Help them to trace the journey with their fingers, verbalising the route as they go along. Allow older children to do most of the planning and problem solving, just give them clues if they get stuck. Encourage them to think about why certain things may be near others, for instance, why a school might be near a housing estate.

## Further ideas
■ Divide the route into small square sections and number them. Let the children take turns to throw a dice and move a number of sections, until they get to the destination.
■ Write the story of the journey and what happens when the children arrive. Mention all the places you pass on the way, making them part of your story. Emphasise the importance of road safety when you have to cross a road.

**LEARNING OBJECTIVES**
**STEPPING STONE**
Describe a simple journey.

**EARLY LEARNING GOAL**
Use everyday words to describe position. (MD)

**GROUP SIZE**
Four or five children.

**HOME LINKS**
Ask parents and carer to show their children simple maps and trace routes on them to show their route from home to your group.

# Busy street

**LEARNING
OBJECTIVES
STEPPING STONE**
Notice differences
between features
of the local
environment.

**EARLY LEARNING
GOAL**
Find out about their
environment, and
talk about those
features they like and
dislike. (KUW)

**GROUP SIZE**
Whole group.

### What you need
Magazines; scissors; adhesive; wheel stencils; paint in one colour; paint brushes; large sheet of card.

### Preparation
Draw a margin around the edge of the card, about 10cm wide. Cut out the wheel stencils from card. Draw the wheels, with lots of spokes to make an interesting stencil shape, and cut them out. Tell the children you are going to make a montage of a busy street, or even a busy town. The street will be in the centre, and the wheel stencils will be all round the edges.

### What to do
Help the children to look through the magazines to find pictures of items that would be found in the street, such as cars, bikes, trees, people, street signs and so on. Help them to cut out their pictures.

Let the children decide where to put their individual cut out pictures and then stick them in place on the large sheet of cars, inside the frame. They can then look for another suitable picture. Encourage them to find a good selection of items. Ask them to find specific things when the montage is complete. Can you find a motorcycle? Can you find a police officer? Can you find a bike? What else might we see in the street? When the montage is finished, ask the children to locate their own cut outs.

Don't worry about trying to make a 'picture'; the idea of the montage is to fill up all of the space in a colourful, busy way. Some of the pictures may even overlap and you can fill in any spaces with paint.

Help the children to place the wheel stencils in the margins and paint in the spaces to match the montage background.

### Support and extension
Let younger children cut one thing out at a time, and stick it on. Give them plenty of help with cutting out and spacing of cut outs on the card. Talk them through the whole activity, ask: Is that one too close to the next one? Is the space too big? Is the space too small? Can we cut a nice clear edge round this car? Give older children clear instructions to remember, 'Look for a car, a bus, two people and a signpost.' When they bring their cut outs to you, ask them which they have managed to collect and which they couldn't find, to check what they have remembered.

### Further ideas
■ Ask the children to make small montages of their own, choosing their own subjects. They could choose a park or school, for example.
■ Cut out different stencil shapes to decorate other artwork, or books. Use montage to make book covers.
■ Talk about what could cause an accident. Show a picture of an area with hazards and ask children to spot all of them.

**HOME LINKS**
Ask parents and
carers to save up
unwanted magazines
to provide pictures
for this activity.

# Baby wheel pizzas

## What you need

Grill or oven; three or four muffins; sharp knife (adult use only); jar of tomato pizza topping; 30g cheese; vegetables – sliced tomato, cucumber, peppers.

## Preparation

Make sure the children wash their hands. Slice the muffins in half. Heat up the grill and lightly toast the cut sides of the muffins, or put them in a hot oven for about a minute. While the muffins are being toasted, grate the cheese.

## What to do

Explain that you are going to make some pizzas that look like wheels. Talk about safety when cooking and make sure everyone understands that they must not touch hot things. Ask them why it's important to wash their hands carefully before beginning to handle food.

Help the children to sprinkle grated cheese on the toasted side of each muffin. Put them back under the grill or in the oven until the cheese begins to melt. Take them out and let the children spoon a little tomato topping over the cheese and then sprinkle more grated cheese on top. Grill or bake until all the cheese has melted. How do the pizzas change when they get hot? What happens to the cheese?

The cheese will be very hot, so make sure the children understand they cannot touch it until it cools down. Show the children how to decorate their pizzas to look like wheels by laying strips of tomato, cucumber, red and yellow pepper (discard the seeds) from the centre to the edge to look like spokes.

## Support and extension

Keep things simple for younger children by making the pizzas yourself and allowing the children to decorate them using the strips of tomato, cucumber and pepper. Older children can be more creative with their decoration, perhaps making spirals or circles, or writing their names using the vegetables.

## Further ideas

■ Invite the children to verbalise the activity in sequence.
■ Play a pizza memory game. Start with 'On my pizza I had cheese'. The next person then adds something and so on.

**LEARNING OBJECTIVES**
**STEPPING STONE**
Talk about what is seen and what is happening.

**EARLY LEARNING GOAL**
Look closely at similarities, differences, patterns and change. (KUW)

**GROUP SIZE**
Three or four children.

**HOME LINKS**
Ask parents and carers to involve their children in simple cookery activities at home.

# Who's on the bus?

**LEARNING
OBJECTIVES
STEPPING STONE**
Manipulate materials
to achieve a planned
effect.

**EARLY LEARNING
GOAL**
Handle tools, objects,
construction and
malleable materials
safely and with
increasing control.
(PD)

**GROUP SIZE**
Four or five children.

### What you need
Card; scissors; sticky tape; crayons; oddments of textured paper or fabric; glue.

### Preparation
Sing through the rhyme together. Let the children decide whether they would like to make a driver or a passenger finger puppet. Cut the card into pieces about 8cm × 4cm, and into strips measuring 2cm × 5cm.

### What to do
Help the children to each draw and cut out a rough shape 6cm or 7cm tall by 3cm wide. Next, ask them to draw and colour their choice of person on one side of the card, adding pieces of textured paper or fabric for clothing and wool for hair and so on.

When the people puppets are finished, make a small ring from one of the strips to roughly fit a child's finger. Attach the ring with sticky tape to the back of the puppet so that the children can then wear their puppets facing into the palm of the hand so they can be wiggled.

Ask the children to work in pairs to have a conversation with their puppets 'talking' to each other. Where are you going on the bus? What are you going to do when you get there? What's your name? Tell me about yourself.

### Support and extension
Let younger children make very simple puppets and provide help with the difficult parts such as sticking on hair. Older children could cut and stick their puppets, rather than drawing and colouring them. Provide coloured sticky paper from which they can cut eyes, mouths, clothes and even buttons.

### Further ideas
■ Make whole families of finger puppets.
■ Encourage the children to tell stories about their journey to school or to a friend's house, using the finger puppets.
■ Make animal finger puppets in the same way, and write a story about a ride on a bus to a farm or a zoo.
■ The children can use the puppets in all areas of their play.

**HOME LINKS**
Let the children
take their puppets
home to show their
parents and carers,
developing their
communication skills
as they play with the
puppets.

# Bus drivers

## What you need
Large space.

## Preparation
Make sure the children know how to stop on command, and how to move around the space without bumping into each other.

## What to do
Tell the children they are going to act out the rhyme by pretending to be the driver of the bus, turning the steering wheel. Can they go straight ahead and left and right, moving at a normal walking space? Now let them try to be the wheels of a bus, rolling on the floor. Can they roll straight ahead, left, right and backwards?

Next, ask the children to stand up again and be the driver working out a pathway. Lead the children in a follow-my-leader line, using slow, controlled travelling actions to establish a pathway. The pathway might be in a long, straight line, with a sudden sharp turn to face a new direction, or a short, zigzagging pathway, a curved or twisting line, weaving in and out, a circle, or a spiral pathway. Choose each pathway carefully.

When the children understand the pathways, ask them to march, hop, run, skip, slither, creep, jump and tiptoe on the different pathways. Invite the children to demonstrate that they understand different words. Who can walk on tiptoe? Who can show us a crawl, a slither, a scurry, a trot, a creep, a march? Who can show us some circle movements – twirl, whirl, spin, roll, twist, curl? Who can show us some pathway words – zigzag, straight, left, right, curve, twist, spiral? End with the children choosing a pathway and level of their own, keeping the speed slow so that they don't bump into each other.

## Support and extension
With younger children, use just a few words at a time, and repeat the same patterns over and over again. Choose different children to be the leader and give them positive encouragement. With older children, aim for high quality movement, and comment positively on really expressive shapes or clear movements so that the other children will observe and mimic. Choose a child to bang a drum to set and change the pace of the activity.

## Further ideas
■ Use percussion instruments to stimulate the movements, for instance, gentle shaking of a tambourine, or short, sharp tapping.
■ Play tightrope walking using chalk to draw long pathways on the ground. Suggest to the children they are balancing on a tightrope and encourage them to tiptoe along the lines.
■ Make spirals out of card by drawing a spiral shape on a circle of card, beginning from the centre and drawing around and around until you reach the edge. Cut along the line and shake the spiral out.

**LEARNING OBJECTIVES**
**STEPPING STONE**
Experiment with different ways of moving.

**EARLY LEARNING GOAL**
Move with confidence, imagination and in safety. (PD)

**GROUP SIZE**
Whole group.

**HOME LINKS**
Encourage parents and carers to take their children to the park or gym sessions to provide opportunities for physical play.

# Listen for the bus

**LEARNING
OBJECTIVES
STEPPING STONE**
Explore the
different sounds of
instruments.

**EARLY LEARNING
GOAL**
Recognise and
explore how sounds
can be changed, sing
simple songs from
memory, recognise
repeated sounds and
sound patterns and
match movements to
music. (CD)

**GROUP SIZE**
Whole group.

### What you need
Home-made instruments (see instructions below).

### What to do
Practise singing and clapping to
the rhyme together. Suggest that
the children play along to the
rhyme using some home-made
instruments.
Make simple instruments:
• cut lengths of dowelling to tap
together;
• fill glass bottles with different
leves of water and tap them with
a pencil.
• hit tins with a  wooden spoon;
• fix sandpaper to two blocks and
rub them briskly together;
• string up several plant pots and
tap them with a spoon or a stick;
• tie spoons to a long length of string, to shake and jangle;
• put dried peas/rice/gravel into empty washing-up bottles or different
shaped and sized containers to shake (ensure that you stick the lids
securely);
• hang different lengths of thin wood from the back of the chair to tap with
a stick;
• secure rubber bands round a brick or box to twang.
Encourage the children to sing the rhyme through using their musical
instruments in time with the rhythm. How can you make sure you begin
together, keep in time, and end together? Which instruments give similar
sounds? Which instrument do you like using best?

### Support and extension
With younger children rehearse plenty of times to establish starting and
stopping on cue before the final version, give clear signals, and keep everybody
watching you as you conduct. Divide older children into smaller groups to
take turns to sing and play, prompt them when it is their turn to play.

### Further ideas
■ Swap the instruments around so that everybody gets the chance to have a
go at one.
■ Make a cassette recording of traffic driving past, speeding up, slowing
down, braking, and ask the children to listen and decide what's happening
from the sounds.
■ Record the children singing and playing, and play the tape back to them.

**HOME LINKS**
Invite parents and
carers in to share
the instrumental
performance of the
rhyme.

# Five Little Ducks

Five little ducks
Went swimming one day
Over the hills
And far away
Mother Duck said, 'Quack, quack, quack, quack,'
But only four little ducks came back.

*Begin verse two with the words:*
Four little ducks…
*Reduce the number of ducks by one with each new*
*verse, until the final verse:*
One little duck
Went swimming one day
Over the hills
And far away
Mother Duck said, 'Quack, quack, quack, quack,'
And five little ducks came swimming back!

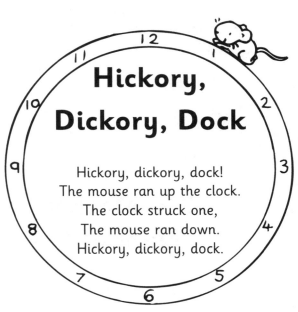

# Hickory, Dickory, Dock

Hickory, dickory, dock!
The mouse ran up the clock.
The clock struck one,
The mouse ran down.
Hickory, dickory, dock.

# There Were Ten in the Bed

There were ten in the bed
And the little one said
'Roll over, roll over'.
So they all rolled over
And one fell out.

There were nine in the bed
(and so on)
*Continue until the final verse.*
There was one in the bed
And the little one said
'Good night'.

# Pat-a-cake

Pat-a-cake, pat-a-cake baker's man.
Bake me a cake as fast as you can.
Pat it and prick it and mark it with 'B',
And put it in the oven for baby and me.

# Old Mother Hubbard

Old Mother Hubbard
She went to the cupboard
To fetch her poor dog a bone.
When she got there
The cupboard was bare
And so the poor dog had none.

# The Wheels on the Bus

The wheels on the bus
Go round and round.
Round and round, round and round.
The wheels on the bus
Go round and round.
All day long.

(Further verses)

The wipers on the bus
Go swish, swish, swish.

The horn on the bus
Goes beep, beep, beep.

The driver on the bus
Goes 'Move down the bus!'.

The mums on the bus
Go chatter, chatter, chatter.

The dads on the bus
Go doze, doze, doze.

The children on the bus
Go rah, rah, rah!

# How many ducks?

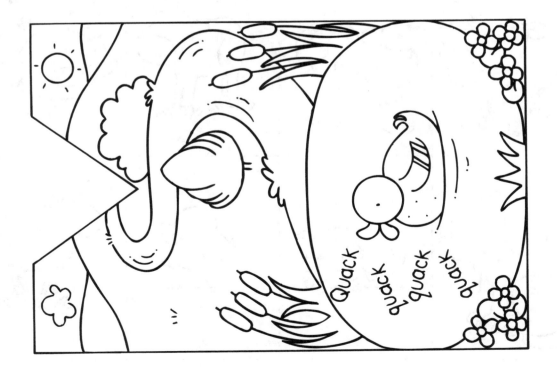

# Mothers and babies

Can you match the mothers to their babies?

# Reach the clock

# Pyjama game

**Photocopiable**

# Time to sleep

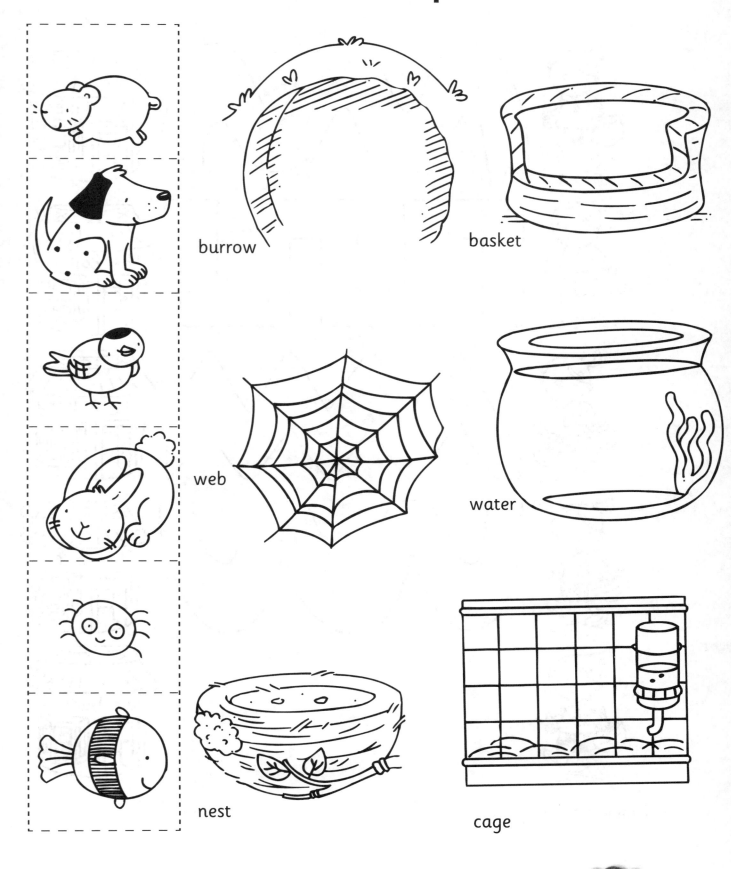

burrow

basket

web

water

nest

cage

# Follow the paths

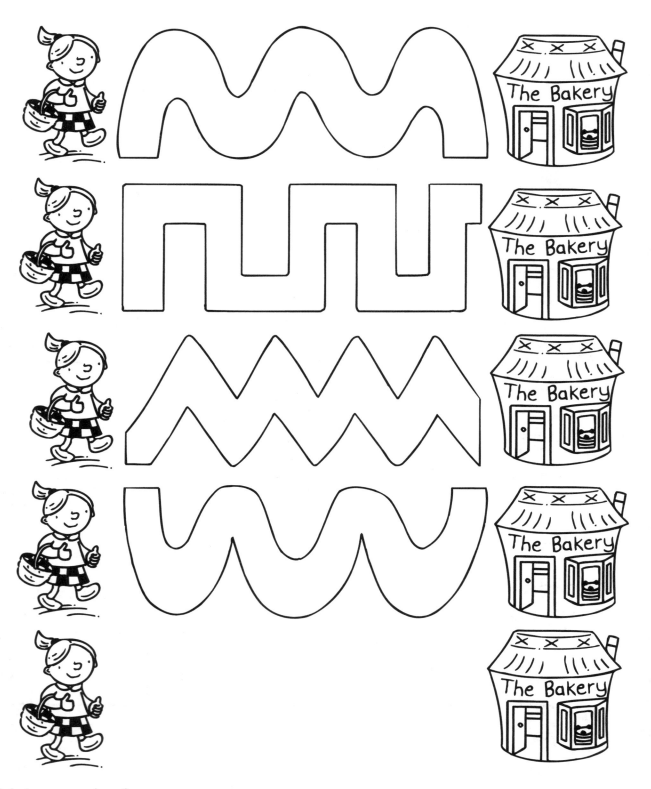

Make a path of your own.

Photocopiable

# How many cakes

Draw one more in each set.
How many in each set?

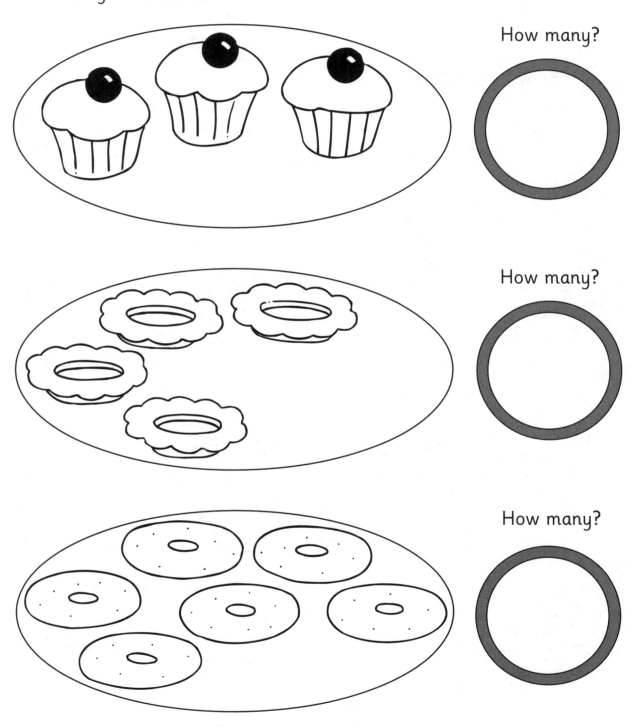

How many?

How many?

How many?

Which is the biggest set?
Which is the smallest set?

# Cakes for sale

# What do we eat?

# Find the shop

Photocopiable

# Who's on the bus?

Who says:

driver

sit down nicely

rah, rah, rah

mums

teacher

move down the bus

doze, doze, doze

dads

chatter, chatter, chatter

children

# Match the wheels

Draw a zigzag pathway to the wheels that match.

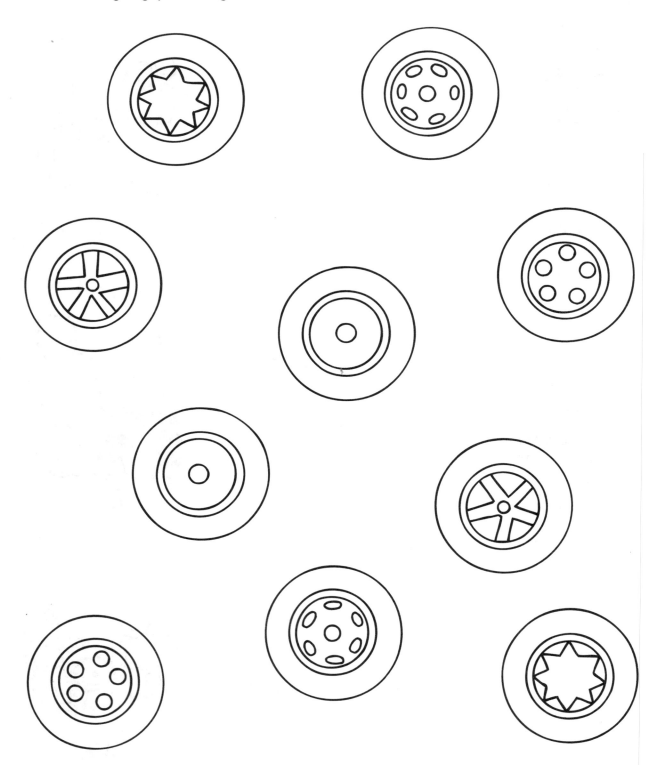

Colour the wheels. Colour the pairs the same.